YOUR MOVE
Logic, Math and Word Puzzles for Enthusiasts

YOUR MOVE
Logic, Math and Word Puzzles
for Enthusiasts

DAVID L. SILVERMAN

Illustrated by Don Oka

Dover Publications, Inc., *New York*

Published in Canada by General Publishing Company, Ltd., 30 Lesmill Road, Don Mills, Toronto, Ontario.
Published in the United Kingdom by Constable and Company, Ltd., 3 The Lanchesters, 162–164 Fulham Palace Road, London W6 9ER.

This Dover edition, first published in 1991, is a revised, slightly corrected republication of the work originally published as *Your Move* by the McGraw-Hill Book Company in 1971. The postscript to the original edition (now irrelevant) has been deleted, and the bibliography and author biography have been updated for this edition.

Manufactured in the United States of America
Dover Publications, Inc., 31 East 2nd Street, Mineola, N.Y. 11501

Library of Congress Cataloging-in-Publication Data

Silverman, David L.
    Your move : logic, math and word puzzles for enthusiasts / by David L.
    Silverman.
       p.   cm.
    Reprint. First published: New York : McGraw-Hill, 1971.
    Includes bibliographical references (p.   ).
    ISBN 0-486-26731-8
    1. Puzzles. 2. Word games. 3. Mathematical recreations. I. Title.
GV1493.S58   1991
793.78—dc20   91-2006
                                                CIP

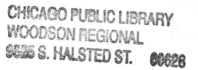
Dedicated to
Martin Gardner
who, more than
any other, is responsible for the flourishing
of the mathematical game tree

Introduction

The author of this book, the reader will discover, has a taste for misdirection and surprise. No out-and-out chicanery, mind you (although his game number 80 comes close to it). It's just that some of the problems that appear most difficult turn out to have simple solutions, and vice versa. Also watch out for bizarre "new" games that are really disguised versions of familiar old games.

As Director of Litton Industries' Problematical Recreations Series, I was impressed with the novelty of his contributions and pleased when he accepted appointment as Chief Consultant. It is largely due to his keen judgment and his bent toward the humorous and the unconventional that the series has acquired a reputation as a forum for new and stimulating puzzle concepts.

This book is divided into two sections. The first consists of eighty solved game problems with the solutions conveniently printed on the opposite side of the problem pages (the author has an aversion to thumbing through a puzzle book in quest of a solution, with the attendant risk of inadvertently reading the solution to a problem not yet attempted). The second part contains twenty unsolved games, which appear rather difficult to me, but which Mr. Silverman assures me will be "duck soup" for some of the gamesters whose names appear in Notes and Sources. Diligent readers will also find many other unsolved "challenge problems" posed in the solutions to the solved problems and in Notes and Sources. The latter section is numbered from 1 to 100 in correspondence with the problems themselves. It is a mine of intriguing research problems, and serious gamesters may find it even more a source of entertainment than the solved problems.

If you enjoy a challenge and don't mind being stumped occasionally, you are bound to have as much fun reading this book as I had reading the manuscript.

ANGELA DUNN

Preface

The objective of this book is to entertain. Any instruction you derive from it is unintended and incidental. And since everyone takes his entertainment in his own style, I wouldn't presume to advise you how to read this collection of game-decision problems, even if I felt there *were* a best way. As a matter of fact, I don't feel that there is. Take my own case: I can recall many challenging problems I attempted to solve for an hour or so, without success. Rather than give up and look at the solutions, I ruminated them for a week or two—while brushing my teeth, walking my dog, having a blood sample taken, or waiting for the waitress to come—and then gave up. Then there is the matter of game number 59. I worked for almost five years to find the general solution, and would have kept at it longer had not wiser heads laid the problem to rest.

On the other hand, there have been problems, such as games 29 and 35, that I found so baffling I turned to the solutions almost immediately. My conscience was not pricked, nor was the beauty of the problems diminished for me in the slightest. The fact is, most problem composers create their problems backward, giving themselves an unfair advantage over their readers. Therefore, if you are the type of reader who starts a mystery story on the last page, feel free to read this book in the same way. You might even enjoy trying to reconstruct the problems from the solutions.

. I would like to acknowledge first my debt to those problem composers whose work I have used in this collection. Insofar as I have been able, I have cited all original sources in the Notes and Sources section.

Next, my gratitude to the gifted group of pioneers who have devised, analyzed, and generalized so many interesting mathematical games over the last two decades. A partial list includes Robert Abbott, Melvin Dresher, Richard Epstein, David Gale, Solomon Golomb, P. M. Grundy, Richard Guy, Piet Hein, Rufus Isaacs, T. H. O'Beirne, Cedric Smith, Roland Sprague, and Edward Thorp.

My personal thanks to those who have played some of the games of this book with me and helped correct or improve my analyses: Lawrence Crane, Richard Field, Sanford Levy, Don May, Steven Muscanto, William Porter, and Al Zalon of the Space Systems Division, Hughes Aircraft Company; Michael Lauder of the Filtron Corporation; Frank Mason of Aerospace Corporation; Norbert Kaufman of the RAND Corporation; Walter Penney of the Department of Defense; Philip Eckman of the Jet Propulsion Laboratories; Solomon Golomb of the University of Southern California; and to Richard Epstein, both for his personal contribution and for writing *The Theory of Gambling and Statistical Logic,* which is certain to be canon among mathematical game enthusiasts for many years to come.

I am grateful to the illustrator of this book (and excellent handicapper), Don Oka, for making the problems live.

Most of all, my thanks to the *sine qua non,* Angela Dunn.

Now, your move.

DAVID L. SILVERMAN

Contents

Part II

"A clear fire, a clean hearth, and the rigour of the game."

—Charles Lamb, *Essays of Elia*

". . . and sometimes reflect with Astonishment upon Games of Whisk, which have been miraculously recovered by Members of the Society, when in all human Probability, the Case was desperate."

—Joseph Addison, *The Spectator,* No. 72

"Herein is shown the power of ingenuity and the triumph of wisdom over strength."

—Phaedrus, *Book I, Fable 13,13* ("The Fox and the Raven")

YOUR MOVE
Logic, Math and Word Puzzles
for Enthusiasts

PART I

Potpourri I

1. MONOCHROME

This is the purest form of POLYCHROME, other versions of which will be considered in due course.

Alternately, two players shade any South American country of their choice, with one restriction. There is only one color available, and since it is traditional among map-makers never to color neighboring countries alike, the rules prohibit the shading of any country which borders a previously shaded country.

The winner is the player who is able to shade the last country—i.e., who is first able to stymie his opponent.

A flip of a coin gives you the privilege of playing first in this first game of the book. Your move!

Solution to **MONOCHROME**

The fact that Brazil borders ten of the thirteen countries of South America, while the two countries with which it has no common border are not adjacent, permits you to win with dispatch.

Shade Brazil. Your opponent is then left with only two choices: Chile or Ecuador. Whichever he shades, you shade the other; the game is over.

Can one guarantee a win by any other opening? Very likely, but not nearly so quickly. Moreover, the analysis required to determine the winning strategy with any other opening is probably sufficiently complicated to require the services of a digital computer.

2. SEVEN NO TRUMP

PLAYER A   PLAYER B

1♣   2♣

2♦   5♦

5♥   5♠

7♠   7NT

This is strictly a two-person bidding game with little resemblance to the game of bridge beyond the fact that the bidding sequence must follow the order prescribed in contract bridge. The "five suits"—clubs, diamonds, hearts, spades, and no trump—are ranked upward in the order given. There are a couple of restrictions on the bidding: (1) The initial bid must be at the one level, and (2) following the first bid, each player has two options: he may either raise his opponent's last bid to a higher level in the same suit (as high as he wishes) or he may raise to any higher-ranking suit at the same level.

The objective is to be the last bidder; i.e., the one to bid 7NT. There are no passes, doubles, or redoubles. The sequence given above illustrates a win for player B. His response to A's opening bid of one club could have been one diamond, one heart, one spade, one no trump, two clubs, three clubs, four clubs, five clubs, six clubs, or seven clubs. He was lucky to win with his two-club response, though it will be seen that neither player had an inkling of the winning strategy.

The fact is that although the first player has a choice of five bids at the one level, the second player will invariably win if he bids optimally. Your opponent draws the first bid by the toss of a coin, and it is up to you to plan your strategy against each of his five possible openings. The problem appears difficult, but you will find it simple enough if you approach it from the right "direction."

Solution to SEVEN NO TRUMP

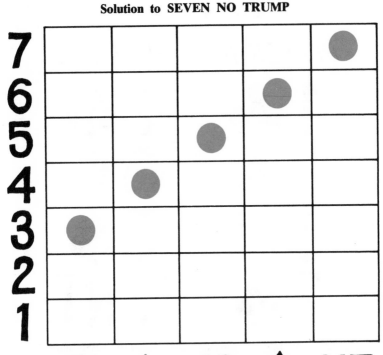

By the rules of the game, a player, according to the diagram, may either move right along a row or up along a column. Thus the five bids indicated by red dots are "safe" in that:

1. When you make a safe bid, your opponent is always forced to make an unsafe bid.
2. In response to your opponent's unsafe bid, you can always raise the contract to a higher safe bid.

Thus the winning responses to the opening bid are:

OPENING BID	1♣	1♦	1♡	1♤	1NT
WINNING RESPONSE	3♣	4♦	5♡	6♤	7NT

The solution of a game problem of this type is generally facilitated by working backward from the winning objective.

A *misere* version of any game is one in which the game objective is reversed. Can you analyze the *misere* version? (The player who bids 7NT loses). For the solution see Notes and Sources.

3. WOOLWORTH (The Five-and-Ten-Cent Game)

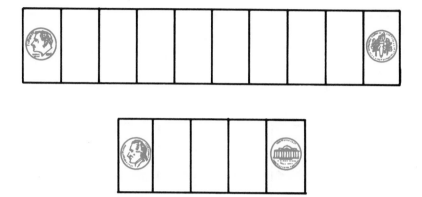

The rules for WOOLWORTH are simple. There are two "tracks" containing five and ten spaces, respectively. At the start of the game, you place a nickel at the left end of the smaller track and a dime at the left end of the other. Your opponent places his nickel and dime at the right ends of the appropriate tracks.

The moves consist of advancing or retreating one of your coins as many spaces as you wish, with the proviso that "jumping" is not allowed. Thus your opponent's coins will always remain to the right of yours. The players move alternately, and the game ends when one of the players is no longer able to move—that is, when he is boxed into his original positions. The other player wins his opponent's fifteen cents.

The flip of a coin gives you the first play. If you are not greedy or imprudent, you can win against any defense. Your move.

Solution to WOOLWORTH

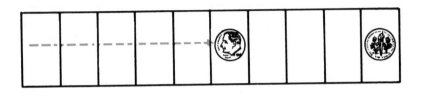

The uninitiated player seems to have an irresistible temptation to move his dime eight spaces to the right, apparently boxing in his opponent's dime. The opponent's winning counter to this opening is to box in your nickel. You now lose after a series of retreats of your dime and advances of your opponent's dime.

The key to the game is to make the gaps between the nickels and the dimes equal. This can be done only by moving your dime five spaces to the right. Henceforth, every move your opponent makes will make the gaps unequal, and your response will make them equal again. Your strategy will be to:

1. Advance N spaces along the same track whenever your opponent retreats N spaces.
2. Advance N spaces along the opposite track whenever your opponent advances N spaces.

The inevitable outcome will be that you will box your opponent into his original positions, leaving him unable to move. Had you made any opening move other than the one indicated, your opponent would have had the opportunity to use the equal-gap strategy against you.

4. YES OR NO?

This is a variation of the game of *Twenty Questions,* with a bit of *What's My Line?* thrown in to make it more interesting.

Red and Black each covertly writes down an integer from 1 to 100. The objective is to guess the other player's number first. Questions may be asked concerning the opponent's number provided they can be answered truthfully with a *yes* or a *no.* A player is permitted to continue asking questions so long as he receives *yes* answers. The first *no* transfers the role of questioner to the opponent.

The conservative *Twenty Questions* strategy of questioning in such a manner as to most nearly equalize the chances of *yes* and *no* answers is most effective in that game. Using it, you can, in only twenty questions, invariably pinpoint any number in the range of one to 500,000. But in the game of YES OR NO? this may not be the best way to proceed.

Suppose you are the first player. What will your questioning strategy be, and how much of an advantage do you feel you have over your opponent?

Solution to YES OR NO?

Your strategy should be quite different from that best pursued in *Twenty Questions*. One way to proceed is to start with the question "Is your number bigger than one?" If you get a *yes* response, your next question will be "Is it bigger than two?" and so on up the line. In this manner, the first *no* answer you receive will pinpoint your opponent's number, which you will promptly guess the next time you assume the role of questioner.

The only way your opponent can win, therefore, is to guess your number on his first round of questions. His chance of doing so is 1 out of 100, so your advantage in this game, as first questioner, is 99 to 1. As the size of the range of numbers increases, the first player's advantage increases correspondingly.

It might be interesting to devise a variant of this game in which a certain amount of falsehood is permitted.

Sidegame:

In *Games of Strategy: Theory and Application*, Prentice-Hall (1961)*, Melvin Dresher posed and analyzed a much more sophisticated search game. The "selector" secretly writes a number from the set (1, 2, 3) and the "guesser" states what he thinks the number is. If he is correct in his first guess, he pays the selector $1; if not, the selector tells him whether the guess was too high or too low, and the guesser tries again. His payoff to the selector is $1, $2, or $3 according to the number of guesses required. It is not difficult to prove that the selector's optimal strategy is to randomly pick 2 with probability 1/5 and 1 and 3, each with probability 2/5. The guesser's best strategy is to first guess 2 with probability 3/5 and 1 and 3, each with probability 1/5. His second guess should never be 2. Selector's expected payoff is $1.80. Selmer Johnson has generalized to guessing sets (1 through n) for n up to 11.

*Reprinted as *The Mathematics of Games of Strategy*, N.Y., Dover, 1981.

5. KING VERSUS KNIGHT

Your opponent with the knight has the objective of putting your king in check. Your objective is to avoid it. He has first move, after which you play alternately, moving your pieces according to standard chess rules. Black wins if he can check you in fewer than twenty-one moves. If you can hold out for twenty move exchanges you win.

There are a large number of possible branches to this game. Perhaps, however, you can devise a strategy that will counter any possible attack by your opponent. Black's two possible first moves are symmetric, so you should start thinking about your first countermove as well as the tactics you will use following the initial exchange. What will your strategy be?

Solution to KING VERSUS KNIGHT

The key to the game is the fact that each time the knight moves, the color of the square he occupies changes. Since he can check your king only by moving to a square of color opposite that occupied by the king, you can foil him by always moving your king to a square of color opposite that occupied by the knight.

There is one catch to this plan. If you are not cautious and allow yourself to be trapped in a corner, you may be put into a position in which you cannot move your king to an opposite color without "walking into check." In such a case you will inevitably lose on Black's next move. To forestall such a disaster, you should always move toward the center of the board. Even with twenty *thousand* moves, Black's knight can never check you.

This simple game suggests a more difficult question: If Black has two knights instead of one, and White is allowed to station the three pieces, what is the smallest number of moves required by Black in order to check the king?

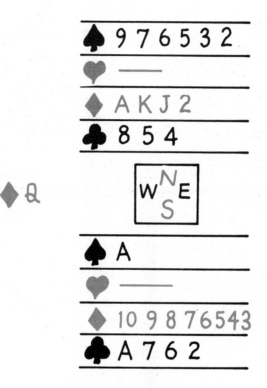

♠ 9 7 6 5 3 2
♥ —
♦ A K J 2
♣ 8 5 4

♦ Q

♠ A
♥ —
♦ 10 9 8 7 6 5 4 3
♣ A 7 6 2

With both sides vulnerable, East opened with a pre-emptive bid in hearts, supported by West after your overcall in diamonds. This interference, however, did not discourage you and your partner from bidding six diamonds, which was passed around.

Had West been obliging enough to lead a heart to the first trick, you could have discarded one of your two losing clubs in dummy and trumped in your hand, assuring the contract. But West was afraid of that possibility and made the more conservative lead of the trump queen.

With two club losers staring you in the face, the outlook is bleak. As South, what is your best play for the slam?

Solution to NOTHING VENTURED . . .

Did you win that first trick in dummy and then pause to plan your strategy? If you did, too bad! Your contract is still makable with a strip and endplay against an opponent obliging enough to hold the king of clubs singleton or doubleton, but the chances are slim and your hopes forlorn.

The plan offering the best chance of success is to play for a 3-3 split in spades, which has nearly a 36 per cent probability of occurring. But to exploit such a split you need three entries to dummy: two to lead and trump spades (after cashing the ace) and the third entry to reach the established spades. West seems to have robbed you of one of your vital entries by leading the thirteenth trump. But reconsider the situation: if you are able to set up and use the spade suit, you will have enough spade winners to discard *all* the losing clubs from your hand. So you can afford to lose a trick in another suit, especially if it is necessary to fulfill your contract.

It *is* necessary to preserve your three entries to dummy. Ergo, you must duck that first trump lead! You will then win the second trick in your hand and play (and pray) for the 3-3 split in spades.

By ducking the trump lead, you risk going down two tricks. But if you fail to duck, you virtually give up all hope of making the slam. The possible profit far outweighs the probable loss.

7. PROTECTING YOUR ADVANTAGE

As White, moving upward on the board, you have achieved a one-man advantage over your opponent. Black, however, is a good player, and unless you are sharp, he stands a good chance of evening the forces and obtaining a draw. Your move.

[Of thousands of checker masterpieces I have seen, this is one of my favorites, both because of the economy of setting and the very unusual theme.]

Solution to **PROTECTING YOUR ADVANTAGE**

The only way of protecting your advantage is to give it up temporarily. You must move your king downward, sacrificing it to the black king, which will then be positioned just barely outside the arena of action. You will then proceed to crown your free man and re-establish numerical superiority by capturing Black's man. With an advantage of two to one your win is now assured.

It requires little time to verify that any other opening move by White will enable Black to draw.

[The sacrifice is a standard checker technique to obtain a profitable exchange or a fatal blockage of the enemy pieces, but this is the only problem, to my knowledge, in which a sacrifice is made solely to gain tempo.]

Sidegame:
An intriguing midget variant of checkers involves the covert placement by each player of three (uncrowned) men of his color on any three of his four bottom squares. Play then ensues as in standard checkers, and not all of the sixteen possible placement combinations result in a draw under best play. In general, optimum strategy requires careful planning. Is there a dominant placement position, or should the players select their initial positions according to a "random mix"?

8. OPEN POKER

The 52 playing cards are spread face up. As first player you pick any five cards you wish. Having seen your selection, your opponent selects any five cards from the 47 remaining. Now you have the privilege of first draw. You may throw away from zero to all five cards and replace them from the 42-card stock as in standard draw poker. Following your draw your opponent may replace as many cards as he wishes from the remaining stock. (He may not draw any of your discards.)

You win if you emerge with the better hand. But since this game is played in completely open fashion, you obviously have an advantage as first player. To compensate, your opponent wins if his hand is either better than yours or of equal rank.

To refresh your memory, a straight flush beats any four of a kind, and two flushes or straight flushes of the same denomination but in different suits rank equally.

You will win this game if you make the right first draw, but think carefully before you make it. What five cards will you select initially?

35

Solution to OPEN POKER

Obviously it would be foolish to select a royal flush, since your opponent would match you with a royal flush of his own, thereby winning.

You must also resist the temptation to pick the four aces and some other card, say a king. Your opponent would respond by picking the four queens and any other card. You would then be in trouble. You could either discard all five cards and draw a jack-high straight flush, in which case your opponent would beat you by drawing a queen-high straight flush, or you could draw so as to prevent him from drawing a queen-high straight flush, in which case he would stand pat and beat you with his four queens.

You will win handily if you start by selecting the four tens and any other card. The best possible hand your opponent can end up with is a nine-high straight flush. You, on the other hand, threaten to emerge either with a royal flush or at worst a ten-high straight flush, and there is no selection your opponent can make which will ward off both threats.

As it happens, there are other winning opening selections involving three tens and various combinations for the other two cards (see Notes and Sources), but the strategy of picking all four tens is most easily shown to be a winning one.

9. THE BEGINNING AND THE END

Here are two vexing decisions in cribbage:

A. On the first hand of the game, opponent with the crib deals you

What cards do you throw into the opponent's crib?

B. With the score tied 100 each, it is opponent's crib again. He deals

What cards do you throw into the enemy crib?

Solution to THE BEGINNING AND THE END

A. You should avoid the temptation of keeping 7778. Keep A777 instead. Consideration of the possible cuts (together with their respective probabilities) indicates that your expected profit (hand value minus three-card crib value) is only slightly less (by about half a point). On the other hand, there is far less risk of a big crib. Equally important, A777 is a superior pegging hand.

Most experienced cribbage players seem to get this right by intuition.

B. This is no time for conservative play. Your opponent will count out hand, crib, and his next hand before you have the opportunity to count a second hand. Therefore, you must keep 3355 and pray for a 4 to be cut.

Any throw other than the deuce and six is tantamount to capitulation.

Sidegame:
An hilarious change of pace for cribbage buffs is "Cribbage Misere" in which each player attempts to put his *opponent* over the 120 mark first. A profound feeling of triumph is achieved by sticking your opponent with a 24-point crib. You win a double point "deficit," of course, by "skunking" yourself.

10. THE RACKS

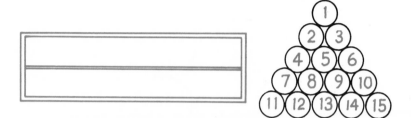

The fifteen numbered pocket billiard balls are to be placed in two racks. The balls must be placed in increasing numerical order, and it is prohibited for three balls to occupy the same rack if the number of one of the three is the sum of the other two. (For example, the 3 ball, the 7 ball, and the 10 ball may not occupy the same rack.)

Your opponent draws first move, which really offers him no choice at all. He must place the 1 ball, and the rack he chooses is immaterial. Now you must place the 2 ball, either in the same rack as the 1 ball or the other rack. The placement will continue in numerical order until one of the players is stymied, in which case his opponent wins. Plan your play.

Solution to THE RACKS

For convenience call the first rack A and the other B. The first player's move is denoted 1A . Your moves are encircled. Now observe the "game tree" that results from your two choices:

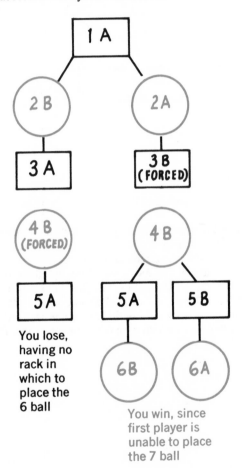

So your winning strategy begins with placing the 2 ball in the same rack as the 1 ball. The game will end after only six balls have been placed. This is your introduction to the tool of the game tree, which you will find very useful in some of the games that follow.

Bridge

11. GREEN LIGHT

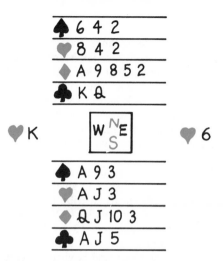

♠ 6 4 2
♥ 8 4 2
♦ A 9 8 5 2
♣ K Q

♥ K   W N E   ♥ 6
   S

♠ A 9 3
♥ A J 3
♦ Q J 10 3
♣ A J 5

N - S VULNERABLE, THE BIDDING:

NORTH	EAST	SOUTH	WEST
PASS	PASS	1 ♦	1 ♥
3 ♦	PASS	3 NT	ALL PASS

Playing South in rubber bridge against experienced opponents, you reach a contract of 3 no trump. The opening ♡K lead, on which East plays the ♡6, is disturbing, though a spade opening might have been even more so. As it is, you have your nine tricks—provided your opponents don't set you before you establish them.

Your choice is limited at this critical first trick. You can win it and hope that West has the ◇K. If you play it this way, you can take out some extra insurance by leading to the ◇A against the possibility of the singleton ◇K with East. If West turns up with the ◇K, your contract is safe, since he cannot run hearts against your ♡J stopper. Of course, if East has the guarded ◇K and another heart to lead through your jack, goodbye contract!

Alternatively, you can duck the first trick with the ♡3 and hope that West follows with another heart, in which case you'll be home free. But West is no duffer and cannot be relied upon to fall for the Bath Coup. He is quite likely to shift to spades, and in that event—even if the spades break 4-3—you'll go down if you lose a diamond trick.

You can't have it both ways. Your move.

Solution to GREEN LIGHT

First decide what it is you fear. Since East followed suit to the heart opening, West has either four, five, or six hearts for his overcall. If West has four or six, you can win the first trick and finesse the ♦ Q with confidence. If East wins with the ♦ K, your opponents can win only three hearts if the distribution was 4-3, and if it was 6-1, East has no heart to return. The danger situation is the 5-2 heart distribution. If West has five hearts, you would dearly like him to continue hearts on the second lead after you duck the first, as that will clear the hearts from East's hand and make the finesse safe.

However, you have already satisfied yourself that ducking with the ♡ 3 will probably induce West to shift to spades. Winning the first trick is also courting disaster if the heart distribution is 5-2 and East has a winning diamond. Is there an alternative? Of course: You have *three* hearts in your hand. The ♡ A and the ♡ 3 are both risky choices. That leaves one card, the ♡ J, and a very good card it is to play! For it banishes West's fear of the Bath Coup and is virtually guaranteed to induce him to continue hearts in the mistaken belief that you have AJ doubleton in hearts. In effect, it gives him the green light to pursue the heart attack. You will win the second heart trick and take the diamond finesse without risk, knowing that if East wins and has a heart to return, the opponents will still win only four tricks.

[Of countless problems in deceptive bridge play encountered by the author, this one stands out as the most ingenious (see Notes and Sources). And what is remarkable is that the almost guaranteed-to-succeed swindle can be arrived at by the simple process of elimination.]

12. TRUMP MANAGEMENT

Having dealt yourself the above bridge hand, you open four hearts, which is passed around. On winning the diamond lead in your hand, you note with regret that dummy is void of trumps. Nothing is to be gained by postponing the drawing of trumps. How you do so is the crux of the matter. Your move.

Solution to TRUMP MANAGEMENT

If the trumps split 3-2, you'll make your contract regardless of how you play them, losing exactly three trump tricks. So you must be prepared for a 4-1 split. In this event, if the $\heartsuit$ 5 is the singleton, the contract is down, period. If the $\heartsuit$ 8 is singleton, a high-trump lead will secure the contract, and if a trump honor is singleton, a low-trump lead will limit you to three trump losers. Since there are three different trump honors, the odds favor a low-trump lead three to one.

However, if you led the 2, 3, or 4 of trumps, you deserve no credit. This novice play would cause you to go down *two* tricks in the event of a 5-0 trump split. Leading the 6 or 7 is the correct solution, since such a lead will result in only a one-trick set in the case of the 5-0 trump split.

Most amateurs miss this one, leading out the $\heartsuit$ J almost by instinct. The more experienced players see the virtue of the low-trump lead, but very few avoid the pitfall of leading the deuce.

13. THE MESSAGE

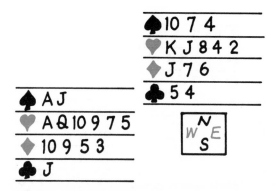

♠ 10 7 4
♥ K J 8 4 2
♦ J 7 6
♣ 5 4

♠ A J
♥ A Q 10 9 7 5
♦ 10 9 5 3
♣ J

N
W E
S

E-W VULNERABLE
THE BIDDING

N	E	S	W
P	4♣	4♠	ALL PASS

Short and sudden! As West you might have entered the auction had the vulnerability not been unfavorable, but you wisely decide to defend. You open with the ♣J, which your partner tops with the ♣K, declarer playing the ♣8. East continues with the ♣A, declarer dropping the ♣Q. What do you contribute to this second trick?

Solution to THE MESSAGE

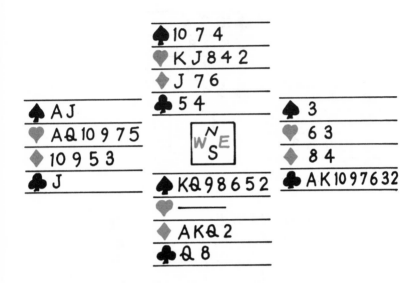

Your play to the second trick will determine your partner's lead to the next one. Therefore you should decide what you want him to lead. A heart, perhaps? No. Declarer is likely to be void in hearts; if not, he has no way of avoiding the loser. If he is in fact void in hearts, a heart lead might be fatal to your cause. But if your partner returns another club at the third trick, you can defeat the contract without difficulty. How do you persuade him to lead another club, knowing that he is aware of the danger of giving declarer a ruff and a sluff? Obviously not by trumping. You must discard a heart or a diamond. A real dilemma, because a low diamond or a high heart calls for a heart switch by East; conversely a low heart or a high diamond calls for a diamond switch.

The solution: Forget about a possible heart trick and discard the ♡A. This unusual play is a clear message to East to make an unusual lead—another club.

One more point. Your partner gets the message and leads another club. South trumps with the ♠K. What do you return after overtrumping with the ♠A? Forget it. You've given away the contract if you made the mistake of overtrumping. Discard instead, and you have two sure trump tricks which, together with the two club tricks, will set the contract.

14. THOSE DIAMONDS

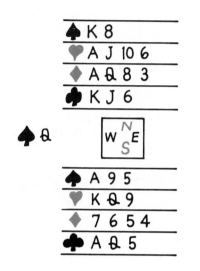

♠ K 8
♥ A J 10 6
♦ A Q 8 3
♣ K J 6

♠ Q

```
    N
 W     E
    S
```

♠ A 9 5
♥ K Q 9
♦ 7 6 5 4
♣ A Q 5

None Vulnerable
The Bidding

S	W	N	E
1♦	P	2♥	P
3♥	P	4NT	P
5♥	P	5NT	P
6♦	ALL PASS		

SOUTH could not think of a better opening than 1 ♦, and it resulted in a shaky small slam contract in diamonds. West's opening lead was the ♠Q, and SOUTH realized immediately that success depended on avoiding more than the one sure trump loser. There are five reasonable ways of playing the diamonds:

1. Finesse the ♦Q. If it holds, cash the ♦A.
2. Cash the ♦A. Lead low from dummy on the next trump trick.
3. Cash the ♦A. Return to hand and lead toward the ♦Q, playing it if West follows with a low trump.
4. Play low from both hands on the first trump trick. Then cash the ♦A.
5. Play low from both hands on the first trump trick. Then finesse the ♦Q.

Probably not more than one bridge player in a hundred would adopt the optimal strategy. As SOUTH, which of the five plans do you favor?

Solution to THOSE DIAMONDS

With K J 10 9 2 of trump missing, there is no hope unless they are divided 3-2. Indeed there are only three distributions which offer a chance of avoiding two diamond losers:

A. $\diamond$ K tripleton with West
B. $\diamond$ K doubleton with East
C. $\diamond$ K doubleton with West

In the fourth case, $\diamond$ K tripleton with East, the contract can be made only by a successful strip and endplay against East, and the chance is too negligible to merit consideration, especially since you have no reason to attribute this holding to East.

In the case of distribution C, your contract is secure regardless of the manner in which you play the trumps, so the decision boils down to determining how each of the five plans fares against distributions A and B, assuming best defense.

STRATEGY	SUCCEEDS IN CASE	FAILS IN CASE
1	A	B
2	B	A
3	A	B
4	B	A
5	A	B

In any 3-2 trump division the $\diamond$ K is more likely to be in the group of three (with probability $\frac{3}{5}$). Therefore, plans 2 and 4 can be discarded immediately. It appears then that plans 1, 3, and 5 are equally sound, since they all work in the case of distribution A and fail in the case of distribution B against best defense. But the defense is not always perfect! There is one plan that offers East the opportunity of going wrong in the case of distribution B. Suppose your first trump lead is the $\diamond$ 3 from dummy. East, holding either K 10, K 9, or K 2 of diamonds, may go up with the $\diamond$ K for fear of having it smothered by your $\diamond$ A on the next trick. This possibility is by no means remote; strategy 5 offers sure success with distribution A and a good likelihood of success with distribution B.

Therefore your best play is to lead a low trump from dummy, and if the $\diamond$ K does not win the first trick, finesse the $\diamond$ Q when you regain the lead. If you correctly adopted strategy 5 and are not a Life Master, then it's only because you haven't had the time.

Chess and Variations

BLACK

WHITE

White is undermanned and in mortal danger. He can achieve a perpetual check and draw, but he would be selling himself short. White to play and win.

Solution to HORS DE COMBAT

BLACK

WHITE

The diagram shows the final checkmate in which White's knight smothers
Black's king. The mating position is obtained this way:

WHITE	BLACK
1. Q to E6 check	K to H8 (a)
2. N to F7 check	K to G8
3. N to H6 double check	K to H8 (a)
4. Q to G8 check	R × Q
5. N to F7 checkmate	

(a) if instead K to F8, Q to F7, checkmate.

FALSE STARTS

1. Q × Q	P = Q check. Black takes initiative.
1. Q × P check	K to F8. White's attack will peter out.

50

16. PATIENCE REWARDED

BLACK

WHITE

White is confronted with a strong threat against which he can again achieve a perpetual check. However he has the initiative, and with proper planning can use it to mate Black's king.

While not exactly simple, the solution is within range of the average chess novice for this reason: against Black's threats, White cannot afford a single waiting move but must keep Black constantly in check until he is able to deliver the checkmate.

White to play and win.

Solution to **PATIENCE REWARDED**

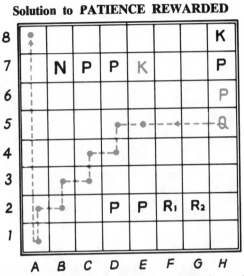

If unhindered by Black's rooks, White plans to navigate the route indicated in the diagram. Each move until the finale checks the Black king along a diagonal. From the start of the White queen's trek, he can handle rook interference without difficulty.

	WHITE	BLACK
1.	Q to E5 check	K to G8 (a)
2.	Q to D5 check	K to H8 (b)
3.	Q to D4 check	K to G8 (a)
4.	Q to C4 check	K to H8 (b)
5.	Q to C3 check	K to G8 (a)
6.	Q to B3 check	K to H8 (b)
7.	Q to B2 check	K to G8 (a)
8.	Q to A2 check	K to H8 (b)
9.	Q to A1 check	K to G8 (a)
10.	Q to A8 check	N to D8 (c)
11.	Q × N check	R_1 to F8
12.	Q × R_1 checkmate.	

(a) If R_2 interposes, Q × R_2 checkmate.
   If R_1 interposes, Q × R_1 check. If R_2 interposes, Q × R_2 checkmate, while if K moves to G8, Q to F8 checkmate.

(b) If R_1 interposes, Q × R_1 check, forcing K to H8.
   Now White moves Q to F6 check, and if R_2 interposes, Q × R_2 checkmate, while if K moves to G8, Q to F8 checkmate.

(c) If R_1 interposes, Q × R_1 checkmate.

52

17. MINICHESS

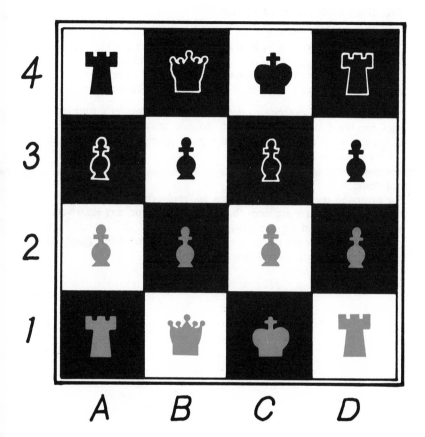

In this abbreviated version of chess, first player has an easy win. To compensate, the second player has the privilege of stipulating which of the four pawns the opener must move (but not the direction of capture).

Black draws first move. You can require him to move either of his rooks' pawns, giving him only one capture option, or his QP or KP, giving him two options in either case.

Only one choice on your part will enable you to win. What will it be QRP, QP, KP, or KRP?

Solution to MINICHESS

Make Black move his Queen's pawn.

	BLACK	RED
If (1)	P × P on A2	Q × P check
(2)	Q to B3	Q × Q checkmate
and if (1)	P × P on C2	P to B3 check
(2)	Q × P	Q × Q checkmate.

It is an interesting exercise to determine the first player's winning strategies for the four openings which do not involve capturing with the Queen's pawn. You will find that the game developments are not always as brief as the ones shown above.

Sidegame:

For diversion try the variant known as "replacement chess." After each capture, the capturer replaces the captured piece on any legal square of his choice. Thus there are always 32 pieces on the board. Jamming your opponent's heavy pieces seems to be the name of this game. Mates, however, usually come quickly and suddenly!

18. GIVEAWAY CHESS

BLACK

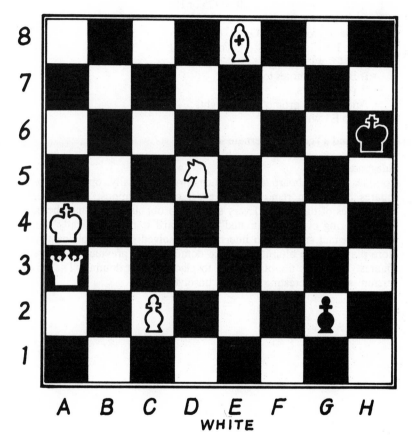

WHITE

In GIVEAWAY CHESS the first player either to be checkmated or to lose all his pieces except the king wins. Captures cannot be refused.

As WHITE you have attained a superiority of forces, but have allowed the black pawn to slip through. If you had your knight at G1, your task would be easy. Now you must play carefully to win. Your move.

55

Solution to GIVEAWAY CHESS

	WHITE	BLACK
1.	Q TO F8 CHECK	K to G5 or H7
2.	Q TO F1	P × Q

If Black promotes to Queen or Rook,

3. B TO F7   Q (or R) × B
4. N to C7 WINS

If Black promotes to Bishop,

3. P TO C4 WINS.

And if Black promotes to Knight,

3. N TO E3 WINS.

Can you find a "cook" (alternate solution)?

Sidegame:

Consider a chessboard from which two diagonally opposite corner squares have been removed and a set of 31 dominos, each covering two squares of the board. Every solver is probably aware that the complete covering of the "mutilated" chessboard is mathematically impossible. This fact suggests an interesting, unsolved game involving two or more players, who alternately place dominos over previously uncovered squares. Winner is the player able to place the last domino. The misere version is also interesting and also unsolved.

19. DON'T MATE IN ONE!

BLACK

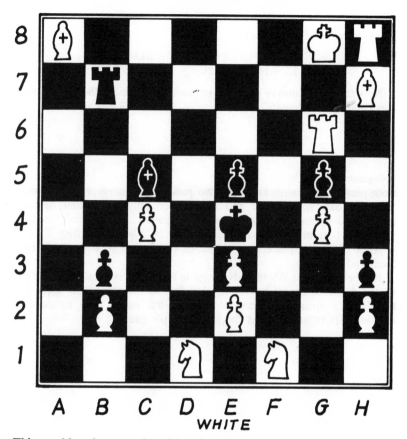

WHITE

This would make a good problem in GIVEAWAY CHESS, except for the fact that WHITE, having the next move, would lose immediately.

Therefore consider this problem as an unusual example of the class of weird puzzles known as Fairy Chess Problems.

It is your move as WHITE. Your objective: move without immediately checkmating Black.

Experienced chess problem-solvers average about two minutes in solving this. Novices (including the ones who conclude that there is no solution) average between fifteen and twenty minutes. If you time yourself, you can thus determine your approximate rating as a chess problem-solver.

WHITE to move and not checkmate.

Solution to DON'T MATE IN ONE!

The elusive, unique solution is

WHITE	BLACK
1. R TO C6 CHECK	1. R × B

Now can you continue in such a manner as to avoid either an ultimate checkmate or a stalemate?

Sidegame:

Both players start with king and two pawns and an empty chessboard. In the initial phase White and Black alternately place their men on unoccupied squares with two restrictions: pawns may not be placed on the top or bottom rows, and kings may not be placed *en prise*.

After the initial placement, White moves first in what amounts to a contrived endgame.

It is believed that White's advantage in moving first is more than offset by the disadvantage of having to play first in the placement sequence. But Black's optimum placement strategy has never been catalogued. Anyone care to analyze this speciously simple game?

20. KRIEGSPIEL

BLACK

In KRIEGSPIEL two players sit back to back, each with his own chessboard. An umpire with a master board directs the game, as each player maneuvers against his opponent, whose position during the game can be inferred only with varying uncertainty. The umpire keeps silent except to advise each player of his turn, following a legal move by his opponent, and to announce:

1. The position where a capture is made (and whether it involves a pawn or a major piece).
2. A check (or checkmate). Umpire will stipulate whether a check is on rank, file, or diagonal.
3. A potential pawn capture.
4. An illegal move. When the umpire announces "no move," the offending player replaces his piece and attempts a different move.

In the endgame, you have whittled Black down to his lone king, while you still retain your king and queen. Your last move was Q TO B2. The umpire announced "Check on the diagonal." That narrows down the position of the Black king considerably. How do you proceed to checkmate Black without risking a stalemate or the loss of your queen?

59

Solution to **KRIEGSPIEL**

Of the various safe lines of play, this is probably the least intricate solution:

RED		BLACK
1. K TO B3	If umpire announces "no move," K is on A4. Red retracts with	
1. Q TO B4 CHECKMATE.		

If, on the other hand, no announcement is made, Black is on D1 and must move to E1.

RED	BLACK
2. TO C2	2. K to F1
3. Q TO D2	3. K to G1
4. K TO C3	4. K to F1 or H1
5. K TO D3	5. K to G1
6. Q TO E2	6. K to H1
7. K TO E3	7. K to G1
8. K TO F3	8. K to H1
9. Q TO G2 CHECKMATE.	

Quicker assured mates may be possible, via, for example:

1. Q TO B4	If this is not an immediate mate, Red follows with
2. K TO D3	Three branches follow, depending upon whether "check" or "no move" is announced, or no announcement is made.

Solvers are invited to find the solution whose longest branch, however many there may be, is shortest.

Checkers and Variations

21. GREEK GIFTS

BLACK

WHITE

As WHITE it is your move in this end position. Though your prospects for procuring better than a draw seem bleak, appearances are deceiving. Consider the possibilities carefully; if you move correctly, you will subject Black to an extremely frustrating experience.

WHITE to play and win.

Solution to GREEK GIFTS

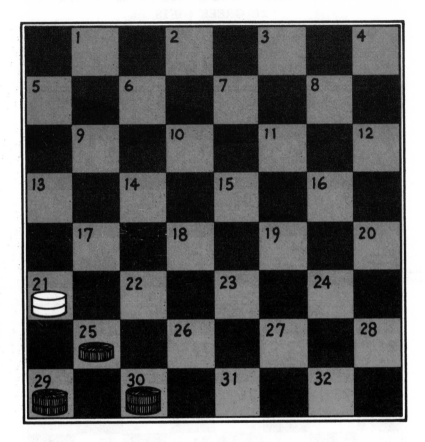

	WHITE	BLACK
1.	13-17	22-25 (otherwise White gains a man)
2.	24-19	16-23 (a Greek gift)
3.	31-26	23-30 (Greek gift number two)
4.	17-21	

White's last move produces the smother position depicted above. Black must move 30-26, giving two pieces back to White who can now trap Black's remaining king.

This problem and its chess analogue (Problem 15) both graphically illustrate the "judo" principle of using your opponent's superior strength as a weapon against him. This theme also occurs frequently in bridge.

22. THE STROKE

BLACK

WHITE

Though there are sixteen pieces on the board, the winning strategy allows Black no options, so there are no alternate branches to complicate the analysis. This is an example of that class of entertaining problems known in checker lore as strokes.

WHITE to play and win in a blaze of fireworks!

Solution to THE STROKE

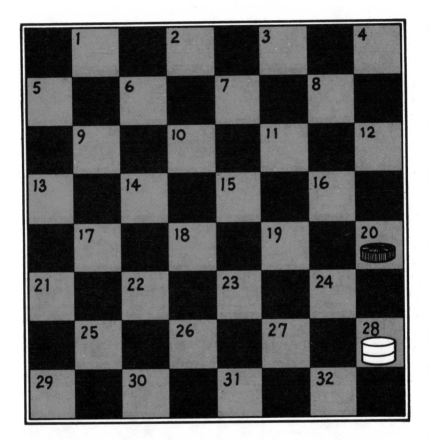

WHITE	BLACK
1. 18-15	19-10
2. 26-23	27-18
3. 22-6	13-29
4. 30-25	29-22
5. 21-17	22-13
6. 6-1	13-6
7. 1-28	

White's last move is a five-bagger that produces the winning position shown above.

23. GIVEAWAY CHECKERS

BLACK

WHITE

Checkers and chess both have *misere* versions that make interesting changes of pace from the standard games (see Problem 18).

In GIVEAWAY CHECKERS, the winner is the first player to lose all his pieces. As WHITE you have a choice of four moves at this juncture. Only one of them is a winner. WHITE to play and win.

Solution to GIVEAWAY CHECKERS

The winning move is 27-23, the same three-for-one shot you would take in standard checkers. This leaves you with two pieces against one and permits you to beat Black easily through your greater mobility. You can now crown your men and chase Black's king, forcing him either to jump your two kings concurrently or to jump one of them in such a way as to leave you with the opposition. (In giveaway, one player has the opposition whenever the other player has what would constitute the opposition in checkers).

The winning principle of giveaway is to achieve an advantage in numbers in the beginning of the game, then to use the greater mobility thus achieved to whittle your opponent down to one king, against two or more of your own. In general you will then be able to force him to pick off your men one at a time.

The same principle holds in GIVEAWAY CHESS, the simplest win involving the reduction of your opponent's forces to the king and a blocked pawn, while you retain a powerful piece or two. You can then usually maneuver your opponent's king to a position from which he must capture all your pieces.

24. THE FOX AND THE GEESE

FOX

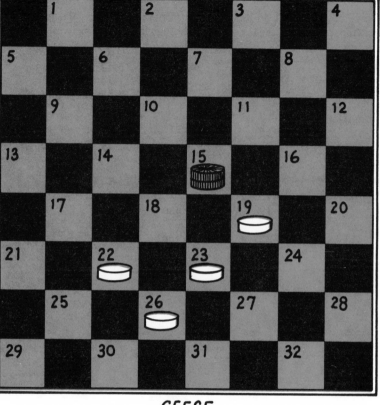

GEESE

In THE FOX AND THE GEESE, one player has four "geese," which move diagonally upward as in ordinary checkers. The other player has the "fox," which moves forward or backward like a checker king. No jumping is permitted.

The geese are originally situated on squares 29-32, the fox's "goal line." The fox starts on any of the squares 1-4, has first move, and the winning objective of reaching his "goal line." The geese win if they can trap the fox before he reaches the bottom row.

The geese have a definite advantage in this game, but must occasionally move quite judiciously to prevent the fox from breaking through.

Following the fox's ninth move, the position is as shown in the diagram. As the geese, what is your next move?

Solution to THE FOX AND THE GEESE

Only one move will do it. Of the four options, 19-16 is the most obvious trap, permitting the fox to break through immediately.

	GEESE		FOX
Trap II	1. 22-17		15-11
	2. 19-16		11-15
	3. 23-19		15-18 Breakthrough
Trap III	1. 23-18		15-11
	2. 19-16		11-15
	3. 26-23		15-19 Breakthrough
WINNING			
PLAY	1. 22-18		15-11*
	2. 19-16		11-15
	3. 23-19	GEESE ARE SOLID	
	*1.		if 15-10
	2. 26-22	GEESE ARE SOLID	

Tic-Tac-Toe and Variations

25. TOE–TAC–TIC

The ancient and popular game of TIC–TAC–TOE is well known to end in a tie (cat's game) with best play. Against a corner opening, the correct response is to take the center square, and any corner will frustrate a center opening. Against any other responses, first player can force a win.

Against a side opening, the second player has a choice of responses that he can convert to a tie. However, as Martin Gardner has pointed out, few TIC–TAC–TOE devotees have taken the trouble to analyze the interesting branches that result from a side opening. There are traps lurking for both players.

In the game of TOE–TAC–TIC (or TIC–TAC–TOE MISERE) the *loser* of the game, if any, is the player who first establishes three of his markers in a row. Play the game a few times with a friend, and you will find that the player with the first move can usually be forced into a loss, most often on the ninth play.

You are under the disadvantage of having to move first. Can you devise a strategy that will insure a tie?

Solution to TOE–TAC–TIC

The key is symmetry. Your first move should be to take the center square and to counter each of your opponent's moves by "reflecting" them through the center. The outcome is inevitable. Either your opponent will lose (though he will have to play suicidally to do so), or the game will end in a tie.

I have heard that the initial play of the center square is the only one that will guarantee a tie against best play, but have seen no proof of it. The game tree is sufficiently profuse to make a complete analysis difficult. But a determined and diligent reader might enjoy settling the question. (Against a corner opening, it seems that the second player can ensure a win by taking a square a "knight's move" away. What about a side opening?)

26. QUICK–TAC–TOE

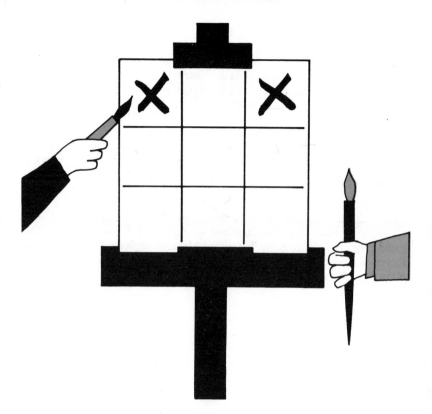

QUICK–TAC–TOE is played in an unusual way. At each turn a player marks as many squares as he wishes, provided they are in the same vertical or horizontal row (they need not be adjacent). The winner is the one who marks the last square.

You are given the dubious advantage of playing second. Your opponent starts by marking the top squares of the first and third columns. Your move.

Solution to QUICK–TAC–TOE

Mark all three squares in the second column and the game is yours. Playing second is not a "dubious advantage" at all. The second player will always win if he follows this strategy: if the first player starts by marking one square, the second marks two to form a connected right angle. If, instead, the first player starts by marking two or three squares, the second player counters by marking as many squares as are necessary to complete either a T, an L, or a cross containing five squares.

The reader should verify that in all cases this strategy insures a quick victory for the second player.

Sidegame:

Felix and Rover play the following perversion of TIC-TAC-TOE: Moves are made as in the standard game, and Felix wins only if the game ends in a "cat's game." If either player completes three in a row, Rover wins. Show without too much difficulty that regardless of who plays first, this is a "dog's game."

27. 3 × 3 × 3 TIC–TAC–TOE

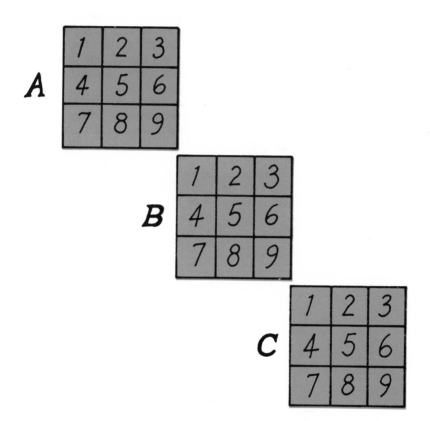

In the $3 \times 3 \times 3$ version of TIC–TAC–TOE, the first player's advantage is insurmountable if he is allowed to take the center square (B5). Therefore the restricted version permits the first player to take any square except B5. The three matrices are to be thought of as tiers of a $3 \times 3 \times 3$ cube. Any three markers in the same line create a win. For example, A4, A5, and A6; or A4, B4, and C4; or A4, B5, and C6.

Given the choice, would you prefer to play first or second? What would your strategy be?

Solution to 3 × 3 × 3 TIC–TAC–TOE

This restricted version enables the second player to win easily against any opening. Whether the first player starts out aggressively or defensively, and regardless of his initial choice of squares, the second player should move into B5. He will then easily counter any threat by the first player, and in so doing will invariably produce a double threat when the first player's attack peters out.

In a more restricted version in which B5 is permanently prohibited to both players, the first player has an easy win. Among other winning openings, he may take A1, creating a starting position in three different planes. If now the second player blocks him in the plane of tier A by taking A5, the first player can take C1, forcing the response B1 and winning with the double threat generated by A7.

All this suggests the real question: Can you devise a set of restrictions that will make an interesting game out of 3 × 3 × 3 TIC–TAC–TOE?

28. 4 × 4 × 4 TIC–TAC–TOE

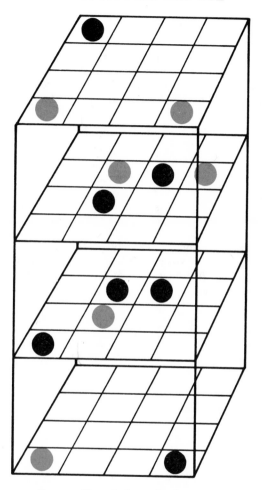

Though the preceding problem led to the implication that 3 × 3 × 3 TIC–TAC–TOE is an uninteresting variation, this is far from true in the 4 × 4 × 4 case.

In this generalization of TIC–TAC–TOE there are four tiers, each four by four. A win is achieved by placing four markers of the same color in a straight line *in any direction*.

In the game shown, Black had the significant advantage of the first move but has left himself in a weak position. If Red can discover the weakness, he has a quick win.

You are Red. Your move.

Solution to 4 × 4 × 4 TIC–TAC–TOE

Letter the four tiers A, B, C, and D from the top down, and number the squares in each tier 1 to 16 from left to right and from top row to bottom. Red has several attacks available, all keyed on squares A14, C14, and D14, and all resulting in a winning double-threat. One of them is shown below. Can you determine the other orders in which the key moves can be made without enabling Black to throttle your attack by means of a counterthreat?

	RED		BLACK
1.	D14	1.	Forces A2
2.	A14	2.	Forces A15
3.	C14	(WINS, THREATENING B14 AND B15)	

Sidegame:
Try this solitaire version: alternately placing chips of two different colors, cover the entire 4x4x4 framework with 32 chips of each color in such a way that no line consisting of four chips of the same color is formed. It can be done!

29. TOUR DE FORCE

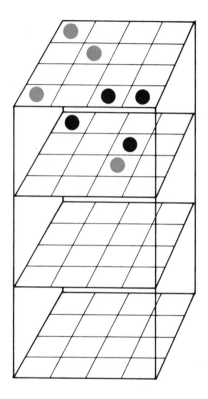

If you suggested to any seasoned player of the game that after only four exchanges of moves, Red is in position to force a win in the above diagram, he would scoff. After examining the set-up, he would be even more convinced that a forced win is impossible. Not only are there no double threats in view; Red is limited even in his possible single threats.

This preamble should alert you to the fact that the winning strategy is not easy to determine. If, after careful study, you are unable to come up with the solution, don't feel badly. I gave up too. In fact, no one who has been given the problem, either by me or by the player who created it, has come close to solving it.

Red to play and win against any defense.

Solution to TOUR DE FORCE

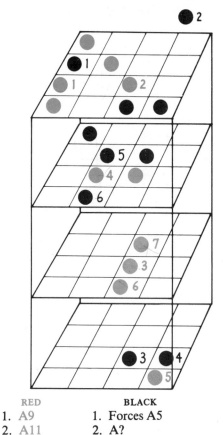

RED	BLACK
1. A9	1. Forces A5
2. A11	2. A?

Black must play on tier A on his second move. Otherwise he will be beaten on tier A by:

3. A10	3. Forces A12
4. A4	4. Forces A7
5. A2 (Wins, threatening A3 and A14).	

Regardless of Black's play on tier A, he will have no counterforces in the development following:

3. C11	3. Forces D11
4. B10	4. Forces D12
5. D16	5. Forces B6
6. C15	6. Forces B14
7. C7 (Wins, threatening C3 and D4).	

It is little wonder that the poser of this gem of far-planned strategy has never lost a game of $4 \times 4 \times 4$ TIC–TAC–TOE playing first and only rarely loses playing second (see Notes and Sources).

Other Board Games

30. HEX

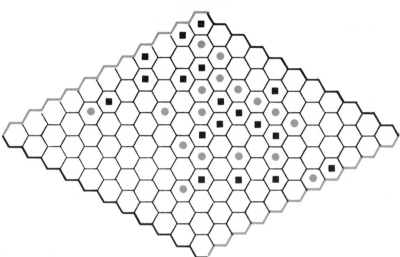

The game of HEX, invented independently by Piet Hein in 1942 and John Nash in 1948, is played on an 11-by-11 rhombic board containing 121 hexagonal cells. Two opposite boundaries are colored red, the other two black, with the corner cells counting for both colors. Red and Black play alternately, capturing cells by placing markers of their own color within any unoccupied hexagon of their choice.

The objective is to create a winning chain of cells, occupied by markers of your color and connecting the two borders of your color. It is obvious that a tie is impossible, since the only way to block your opponent is to create a winning chain yourself. It follows from this and the fact that the possession of an extra cell of your color cannot possibly damage your cause, that the first player has the winning advantage. However, unlike the similar game of BRIDGE–IT, nobody has come close to analyzing the winning strategy for HEX.

In the game illustrated above, Black had first move and appeared to be headed for victory until his last move. Red, whose turn it is to play, can assure a win by capturing the right cell.

In the game that was actually played, Red made a different move, which generated a sequence of forced moves by Black, but eventually petered out, giving Black the initiative, and Black went on to win.

Taking the game back to the critical point, Red should examine carefully the pros and cons of each candidate cell before deciding on the optimal capture. Your move.

Solution to HEX

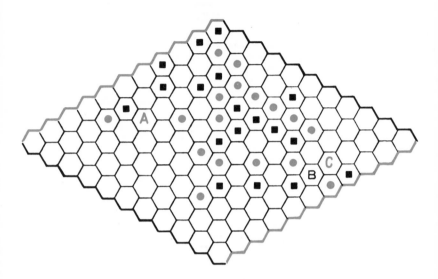

Red should capture the cell marked A. Having done so, he cannot be blocked from his left boundary. Moreover, if Black allows him to capture cell B, Red's Southern forces will have completed a chain from one Red boundary to the other, with only the formality remaining of helplessly permitting Red to capture one of two cells in each of his "double threats."

Black is forced, therefore, to capture cell B, and Red administers the *coup de grâce* by taking cell C, uniting his Northern and Southern forces in an unblockable chain of double threats.

[It is conceivable that Red can maintain his winning advantage by capturing a cell other than A, but I have tried to analyze his other possible lines and have found none that could not be defeated by proper defense on the part of Black.]

31. MINIHEX

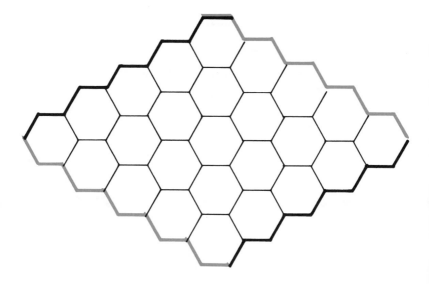

In the miniaturized 5-by-5 version of HEX, the first player can win easily, even if barred from capturing the center cell on his first move. Play a few games and try to determine which initial moves guarantee a win.

To make the game fairer, you and Black have agreed on the following rule. You will bid alternately until either player passes, terminating the auction. The bids must be in ascending order, but not necessarily consecutive in value. The auction might proceed 3–5–9–pass.

The winner of the auction—the highest bidder—must initially place a number of enemy counters equal to the amount of the highest bid on any cells of the highest bidder's choosing. Having placed the enemy counters, it is then his move, and play proceeds as in standard HEX.

A flip of the coin gives you first bid. Success or failure will be determined by the amount of that bid. How many cells of your own selection are you willing to spot Black before making your first move?

Solution to MINIHEX

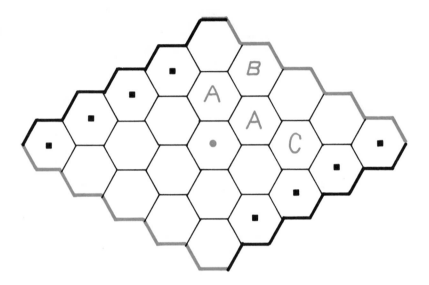

The magic number is eight. If your opening bid is less, Black will bid eight and beat you. If you bid more, he will pass and beat you.

The diagram shows how you will position Black's eight counters should he decline to make a higher bid. You will then occupy the center cell and will have free access to both of your boundaries. By symmetry we need consider only your Northeast boundary. Should Black's response be other than B, you will win by taking one of the two A cells. If Black captures cell B, you will break through by capturing cell C.

As an interesting exercise, show that if Black is spotted nine counters, he can win against any strategy.

32. GO

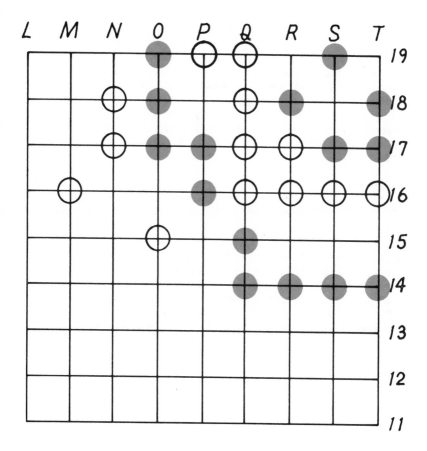

Here is a position that will probably not trouble a seasoned GO player, but one in which the average novice is likely to go wrong.

Play in other segments of the board has been fairly uneventful. As Red your attention is occupied by threatening developments in the Northeast. Your move.

Solution to GO

Your move should be P 15. Rather than concentrate all effort on averting the threat to your five stones in the Northeast corner, you should play so as to rescue your men on O 17, O 18, O 19, P 16, and P 17. In so doing, you will mount a strong counterthreat to the black stones in the Northeast.

If you chose to play R 19 instead, you would be able to save your corner group, but at the expense of losing your group on the left, and you would not realize the advantage of the counterthreat achieved by P 15.

Sidegame:
GO-MOKU is described on the following page, and an exciting game it is. But two players who play a long series will usually find themselves using similar attack and defense strategies repeatedly and for them the author offers an interesting variant: ROKU-MOKU. The rules are the same with two exceptions: The first player to form *six* in a row is the winner, and each player at his turn has *two* moves, except at the second player's first turn, when he has *three*. Try it a few times.

Whence comes the name of this game? Well, the Japanese words for 1, 2, 3, 4, 5, and 6 are "ichi," "ni," "san," "shi," "go," and "roku." Can you quickly show that SHI-MOKU (with single moves) is a trivial game?

33. GO–MOKU

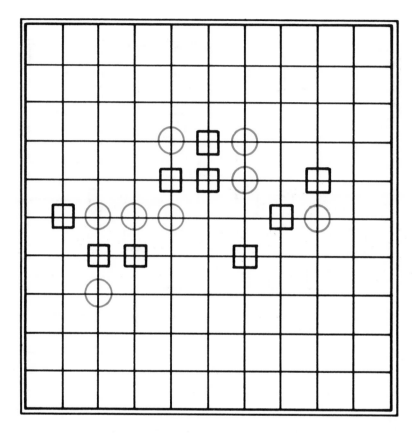

GO–MOKU is played on a standard GO board comprising a square grid of 19 by 19 lines. The objective is to capture five adjacent grid points in a straight line, oriented either vertically, horizontally, or diagonally.

A player who succeeds in capturing four adjacent points in a line with both ends unoccupied (an "open 4") has a win, since his opponent cannot block both ends in one move.

In the game depicted above. Black has established an open 3, which he would be happy to extend to an open 4, should you give him the opportunity. You could block it and see how his attack develops (and you wouldn't have long to wait). But you can do better.

Red to play and win.

Solution to GO–MOKU

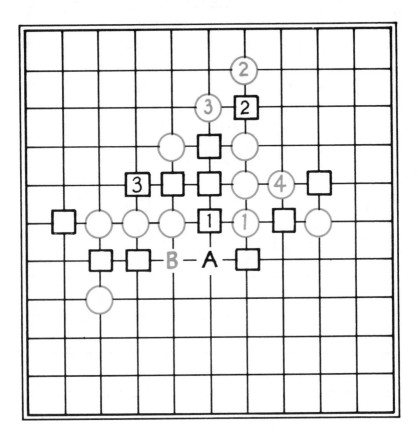

If you blocked Black's open 3, he would play A, forcing you to play B. Then by playing the square marked 1, he would establish a winning open four.

Instead, you must attack immediately by playing circle 1. His response of square 1 is forced. You continue to force him at moves 2 and 3 and your fourth move establishes your own open 4.

A clear case in which attack is not merely the best, but the *only* defense.

34. CONNECTO

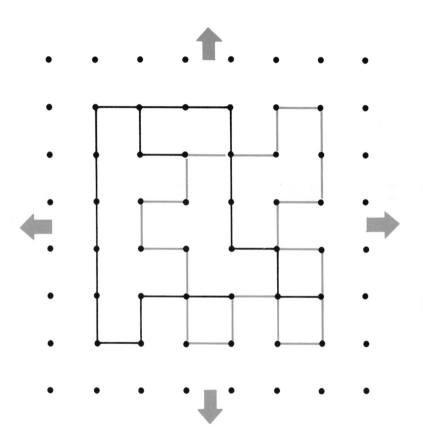

In the game of CONNECTO, two players alternate in joining adjacent points, horizontally or vertically, on an infinite rectangular lattice, one using black lines for his connections, the other, Red. The winner is the first to enclose a region of any shape by a boundary composed of his color only. The Red player has won above.

You have undertaken to play CONNECTO against an experienced player. The flip of a coin gives your opponent the first move—obviously an advantage. Can you, nevertheless, devise a simple strategy that will prevent him from winning?

87

Solution to CONNECTO

It is not difficult to see that every closed boundary must contain at least one pair of perpendicular segments forming an L. Consequently, you can avoid defeat by completing each of your opponent's potential Ls, drawing the foot whenever your opponent makes a vertical connection and the upright whenever your opponent makes a horizontal one.

As suggested in Notes and Sources, the triviality of the game disappears if CONNECTO is generalized to a *three*-dimensional lattice. Here one is tempted to believe that first play confers a winning advantage.

Sidegame:
The L Strategy is ruled out if each move entitles you to make *two* connections. Playing that variation, does second player still have available an unbeatable defense strategy?

35. FORTRESS

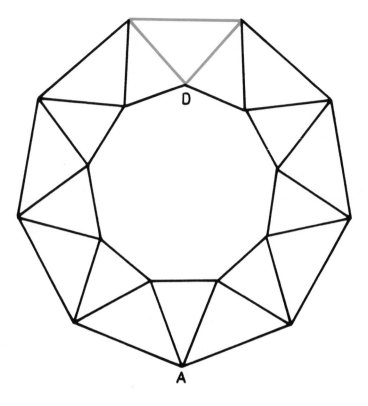

Two opponents alternately move from an intersection to an adjacent intersection. The defender, originally situated at D is confined to the three intersections of the "fortress," outlined in red. The attacker, starting at point A, has first move and operates only under the constraint that once having made a particular move, the path between those two intersections is barred in future. This restriction eliminates the need for a time limit.

The objective of the attacker is to enter the fortress on the same vertex that the defender is occupying, thus "capturing" him. If the attacker succeeds, he wins. If he enters an unoccupied vertex of the fortress, he loses, since the defender can then capture him. The attacker loses also if he is negligent enough to stymie himself by moving into a *cul-de-sac*.

Apparently a difficult game to analyze. Whose role would you prefer, and what would be your strategy?

Solution to FORTRESS

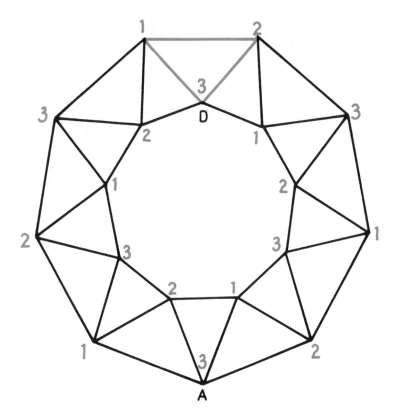

Number the vertices as shown. Working backward from the fortress, it can be seen that a winning strategy for either player is to move always to a vertex labeled with the same number as that which his opponent presently occupies.

Since the initial positions are both labeled 3 and the attacker moves first, the defender has the winning advantage. Therefore take the defender's role, adopt the equalizing strategy, and you will inevitably capture the attacker, if he doesn't force himself into a *cul-de-sac*.

If the defender were required to move first, the attacker would have the winning advantage using the same strategy. Note that any departure from the equalizing strategy permits the opponent to seize the advantage.

Map Games

36. BICHROME

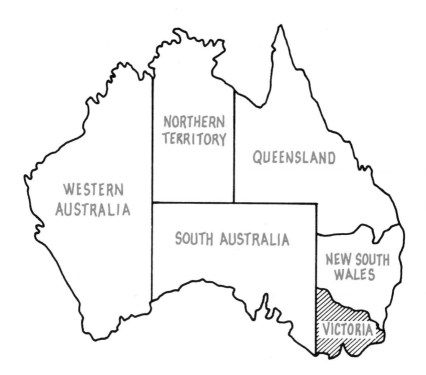

In BICHROME the principle of play is identical to that of MONO-CHROME (see Game 1) except that each player has the option of using either of two shades on each move, say red or black. He may shade any Australian province with the proviso that it must not have the same color as any previously shaded province with which it shares a common border.

The object is to stymie your opponent, the winner being the player who makes the last legal move. In the above game, your opponent has drawn first move and has chosen to color Victoria black. You have eight different options for your reply. You can shade South Australia or New South Wales red, or you can shade Queensland, Northern Territory, or Western Australia with either of the two colors.

Only one of the eight options will insure you a win. Your move.

Solution to BICHROME

WESTERN AUSTRALIA	NORTHERN TERRITORY	QUEENSLAND	NEW SOUTH WALES	VICTORIA
SOUTH AUSTRALIA				

Reduced to a simpler, rectangular map, the Australian provinces show an interesting symmetry that facilitates the solution considerably.

Shade Western Australia red . This puts South Australia out of play and limits your opponent's options to four. Depending upon which he chooses, you will stymie him on your next move by shading Northern Territory black or New South Wales red , whichever of the two plays is legal.

Had you made any other response to your opponent's opening move, it is simple to verify that in each of the seven cases he would have been able to seize the initiative. It will be a profitable exercise for you to work out your opponent's winning second move in each case. It happens that it always involves shading with the color opposite that used in your response.

Finally, it should be noted that the symmetry of the provincial boundaries dooms the first player to defeat in Australian BICHROME. To his openings of Victoria, New South Wales, or South Australia you respond with Western Australia, Northern Territory, or Queensland, respectively, and vice versa. In all cases use the opposite color. You can readily verify that these will be winning responses.

37. TRICHROME

This time you are playing the three-color game on a map of thirteen western states. Your opponent started by shading California, and after five moves only two of the three colors have been used (indicated above by numbers).

Normally it would take some involved analysis to determine your optimum move, but your opponent has left you a configuration in which you can assure yourself a win without the necessity of following the numerous branches along which the game might proceed.

Study the map carefully.

Solution to **TRICHROME**

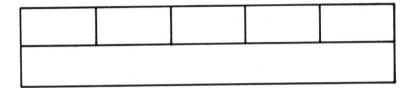

The topological chart above bears a remarkable resemblance to that of the Australian provinces (see preceding game). Moreover, none of these six states can legally be shaded with color 2. Thus, if you can reduce the game to these six states with your opponent required to play first, you will have reduced the game to Australian BICHROME, to which you already know the winning responses.

Your winning move is to shade Oregon with color 3. This makes Nevada unplayable, and your opponent is forced to choose from six losing openings in the equivalent of Australian BICHROME.

38. CONTACT

Here we have South America again, but the objective is quite different from what it was in MONOCHROME. In this two-man game, after the first player picks a country, each succeeding play involves selecting a previously unchosen country sharing a common border with the country your opponent has last selected. The player with the last legal move is the winner.

You draw first move and can win, either by stymying your opponent or by arranging to have all thirteen countries played. Naturally your opponent will try to prevent this by stymying you.

This is a tough one. Your move.

Solution to CONTACT

Brazil turns out to be a winning opening, as it was in the antithetical game of MONOCHROME. The winning lines against each of Black's possible responses are illustrated in the game tree below. The branches vary in growth from sparse to luxuriant.

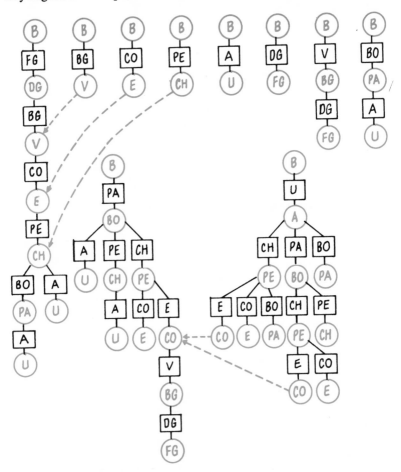

Are there any other openings that will win against any defense? Probably, but if you want to find them, you'll have to do some tree culture on your own.

39. CONTACT MISERE

THE SEVEN KINGDOMS OF
IRELAND, A.D. 500-900

Using a map of ancient Ireland, you have first move in the misere version
of CONTACT. The objective is to be stymied, or—to put it differently—
the loser is the last player able to move. As in CONTACT, each play
after the first must be a previously unplayed kingdom sharing a border
with the opponent's preceding play. Note that since you have first move,
you will lose if all seven kingdoms are played. Only one kingdom will
assure you a win. Can you find it?

Solution to CONTACT MISERE

Using the following abbreviations, the solution is arrived at by the process of elimination:

Ailech: A   Mida-Brega: B
Airgialla: R   Muma: M
Connachta: C   Ulaid: U
Laigin: L

The tree below shows that six opening moves are losers. Those branches that terminate in Black squares all involve continuations in which Red is stuck with the last kingdom:

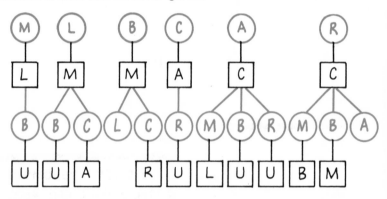

That narrows the field to Ulaid, which is indeed a winning opener. If Black responds with Airgialla, Red counters with Connachta. If Black responds instead with Mida-Brega, Red counters with Muma. In either case Black will be saddled with the last play.

Problems in Elementary Game Theory

40. FIVE OR ONE

You and Black spend an afternoon playing a matching game. Simultaneously you each display a coin, either a penny or a nickel. If both coins are of the same denomination, you win Black's coin. If they are different, Black wins your coin.

If you adopt a "pure strategy" such as playing the penny every time, Black will play a nickel every time, winning your penny on each round. On the other hand, if you know that Black will play a nickel every time, you can do likewise, winning his nickel on each round. Thus neither of you can afford to play a pure strategy, but must mix plays according to some random procedure. What are the optimal strategies, and who has the advantage?

Solution to FIVE OR ONE

BLACK PLAYS

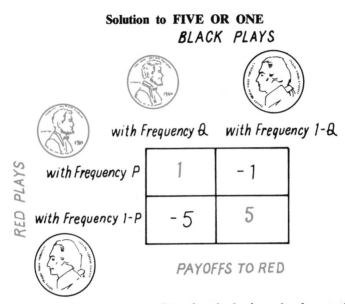

with Frequency Q.   with Frequency 1-Q

RED PLAYS

	with Frequency Q	with Frequency 1-Q
with Frequency P	1	-1
with Frequency 1-P	-5	5

PAYOFFS TO RED

This game can be analyzed readily using the basic tools of game theory. The 2-by-2 array above is your "payoff matrix." If you play the penny with probability P and Black plays his penny with probability Q, your expectation on a given round is given by the formula $E = PQ(1) + P(1-Q)(-1) + Q(1-P)(-5) + (1-P)(1-Q)(5)$.

Simplifying, $E = 12PQ - 6P - 10Q + 5$, which can be written in the form $E = 12(P - \frac{5}{6})(Q - \frac{1}{2})$.

Now if you choose $P = \frac{5}{6}$, you can guarantee that $E = 0$, while if you use a larger value of P, Black can give you a negative expectation by using a Q of 0. Conversely, if you choose a value of P smaller than $\frac{5}{6}$, Black can counter by choosing $Q = 1$, again providing you a negative E. Black, for his part, can also guarantee you an expectation of 0 by choosing $Q = \frac{1}{2}$. If he should deviate from this choice by choosing either a larger or a smaller value for Q, you can assure yourself a positive E by letting $P = 1$ or 0, respectively.

Thus the optimal strategies involve a P of $\frac{5}{6}$ for you and a Q of $\frac{1}{2}$ for Black. Since your expectation is zero under optimal play, the game is a fair one.

In practice, the strategies can be implemented by Black's flipping a coin and playing the nickel if it comes up heads and the penny if it comes up tails. You should roll a die and play the nickel if one spot comes up, the penny otherwise.

Against an uninitiated opponent you could assume either player's role, and by observing the frequency of your opponent's plays, alter your own in a manner guaranteed to provide you a profit in the long run.

41. HIGH STAKES

BLACK NUMBERS

	1	**2**	**3**	**4**	**5**	**6**
A	LOSE $5	LOSE $10	LOSE $1	LOSE $10	WIN $2	LOSE $1
B	LOSE $1	WIN $2	LOSE $10	WIN $7	LOSE $5	WIN $20
C	WIN $2	WIN $7	LOSE $5	LOSE $10	LOSE $10	WIN $7
D	WIN $7	WIN $20	LOSE $1	LOSE $1	LOSE $1	WIN $2
E	WIN $20	WIN $7	LOSE $10	WIN $7	LOSE $1	LOSE $10

RED LETTERS (left margin label)

PAYOFFS TO RED

In the preceding game, involving a 2-by-2 payoff matrix, it was some-what difficult to compute the optimal mixed strategies for the two players.

The game of HIGH STAKES has a 5-by-6 payoff matrix. Yet you will find that its solution is simpler with the application of plain logic.

As Red, you write one of the five letters A, B, C, D, or E on a piece of paper. Black writes 1, 2, 3, 4, 5, or 6, and the letter and number are displayed simultaneously.

The matrix above gives your payoff for each of the thirty possible events. For example, if you write down the letter E, you will win $20 from Black if he writes a one, but will lose $10 to him if he writes a three.

Assuming that each player is aware that his opponent will play opti-mally, what is your best strategy?

Solution to HIGH STAKES

Note first that Black will never write a 6, because regardless of the letter you choose, he will fare better—or equally well—by choosing 3. From Black's point of view, the play of 3 dominates the play of the 6. Effectively, the payoff matrix is reduced to 5-by-5 dimensions by the logical deletion on Black's part of the 6th column.

Now, although your play of D did not dominate C in the original matrix, it does in the reduced matrix, so the matrix is further reduced by your deletion of the C row. Likewise E dominates B, so the B row should be deleted, leaving a 3-by-5 matrix (A, D, and E vs. 1, 2, 3, 4, and 5).

In this 3-by-5 matrix, Black should delete column 2, which is dominated by column 4, and column 5, which is dominated by column 3.

The original matrix is now reduced to 3-by-3 dimensions. Row A should be deleted, since it is dominated by row D Black should now delete columns 1 and 4, both dominated by column 3. Since Black has reduced his six choices to the single choice 3, your optimal play is D, resulting in the loss of $1.

Though your best play results in a loss, you should not deviate from the pure strategy D, since such a deviation will result only in an equal or greater loss if Black plays optimally.

Using the dominance principle, you have arrived at the mutually optimal play combination D 3 by paring down the original 5-by-6 matrix to a 1-by-1 matrix, arriving at the "saddle point," D 3. An experienced game theorist would have located it more quickly by noting that D 3 is simultaneously a row minimum and a column maximum.

42. SEALED BIDS

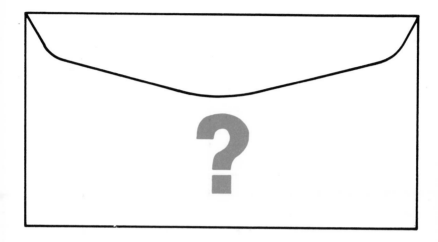

Red and Black each antes a nickel. Now each competes for the antes by writing down a sealed bid. When the bids are simultaneously revealed, the high bidder wins the antes and pays the low bidder the amount of his low bid. If the bids are equal, Red and Black split the pot.

How much do you bid, Red?

Solution to SEALED BIDS

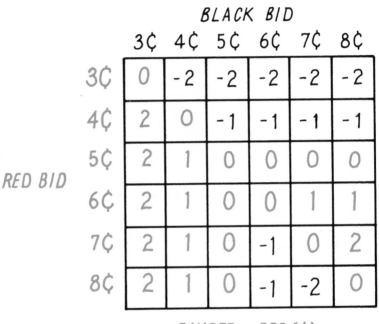

BLACK BID

PAYOFF to RED (¢)

Observing the abridged payoff matrix, it is clear that the only bids which are guaranteed not to produce a net loss are 5¢ and 6¢. Thus bidding either 5¢ or 6¢ is an "optimal" strategy. With either bid, you can't lose.

However, some optimal strategies are sometimes better than others, and that is true in the case of SEALED BIDS. The 6¢ bid clearly dominates the 5¢ bid and is therefore best. If the other player is foolish enough to make an unduly high bid, the 6¢ bidder will win 1¢, while the 5¢ bidder will break even. In all other cases the two bids fare equally well.

The result holds true regardless of the number of players (assuming that the high bidders divide the pot and the liabilities equally). Always bid one unit more than the ante.

43. MORE OR LESS

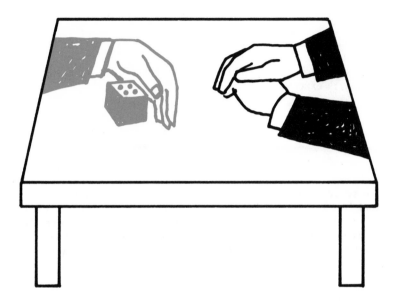

Red and Black play a dice variation of **MORRA** in which each selects a number from one to six and positions his die to show that number on its upper face, concealing the die from his opponent's view.

Red now announces his estimate of the total number of spots showing on the two dice. Black has two options following Red's announcement. He may either say "more" or "less." The dice are uncovered, and Black wins if he is correct. Otherwise Red wins. For example, if Red announces "five" and Black responds "less," Black wins if the actual total is two, three, or four and loses otherwise.

This game has a large, unwieldy payoff matrix. However, if you begin by miniaturizing the game to one involving the selection of either 1 or 2, and then consider the 1, 2, or 3 version, you should be able to generalize to the 1-to-6 game, and, indeed, to the 1-to-N game for arbitrary $N > 1$.

What is Red's optimal strategy?

Solution to MORE OR LESS

Analysis of the miniaturized versions suggests the conjecture that in the generalized game, in which each player may choose any number from 1 to N(N > 1), the game is fair, and a pair of optimal mixed strategies is:

Red: select 1 or N with equal frequency, and always announce "N + 1."

Black: with equal frequency, select 1 and say "less" or N and say "more."

The symmetric payoff matrix indicates that under these strategies, each player's expectation is zero.

	BLACK	
	1 "Less"	N "More"
RED 1 "N + 1"	B	R
N "N + 1"	R	B

To prove these strategies optimal, let x denote a selection between 1 and N and "A" and "B" announcements less than or greater than "N + 1," respectively. The matrices below indicate that if either player departs from his optimal strategy, while the other player sticks to his, the latter will always retain at least 50 per cent probability of winning.

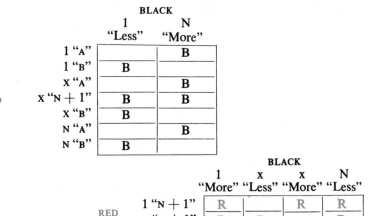

	BLACK	
	1 "Less"	N "More"
1 "A"		B
1 "B"	B	
x "A"		B
RED x "N + 1"	B	B
x "B"	B	
N "A"		B
N "B"	B	

	BLACK			
	1 "More"	x "Less"	x "More"	N "Less"
RED 1 "N + 1"	R		R	R
N "N + 1"	R	R		R

Thus in the dice version of MORE OR LESS, Red should pick only 1 or 6 according to the flip of a coin and announce "7" in either case. This assures him of breaking even in the long run and making a profit if Black does not play optimally.

Is there a meaningful game if the value of N is not limited?

106

44. A THREE-MAN GAME

Three strangers, Black, Gray, and Red (you) share a few rounds of drinks at the Nineteenth Hole of the country club. A mutual friend drops by and suggests the following diversion: the three of you will play a variation of MORRA in which "Mr. Prime" has the option of holding up one finger or five, "Mr. Square" holds up one finger or nine, and "Mr. Otherwise" holds up two fingers or nine. Mr. Prime wins if the total number of fingers (displayed simultaneously) is prime. Mr. Square wins if the total is a square. If the total is neither prime nor square, Mr. Otherwise wins. The two losers must pay the winner's tab.

The assignment of roles is made by matching coins. Odd man has first choice of role. The remaining two roles are assigned by coin matching between the other two players.

It is to be assumed, since the three players are strangers to each other, that there will be no collusion. Also, since game theorists will discover that this game has no stable solution, it should be regarded as a one-time affair. Finally, you should assume that your opponents will play optimally.

You are lucky on the coin matching, throwing tails, while both opponents throw heads, What role do you select, and how many fingers should you display when the game is played?

Solution to A THREE–MAN GAME

Mr. Prime	Mr. Square	Mr. Otherwise	Winner
1	1	2	Mr. Square
1	1	9	Mr. Prime
1	9	2	Mr. Otherwise
1	9	9	Mr. Prime
5	1	2	Mr. Otherwise
5	1	9	Mr. Otherwise
5	9	2	Mr. Square
5	9	9	Mr. Prime

Take the role of Mr. Square, and the game is yours. The analysis is based on the fact that both your opponents have clearly dominant plays, which they are certain to make under the assumptions of the problem.

Mr. Prime wins by displaying one finger any time he would have won with five, and in one additional case. Hence he will display one finger.

Mr. Otherwise wins with two fingers whenever he wins with nine, and in one additional case. He will therefore display two fingers.

Knowing this, you as Mr. Square will receive a free ride at the Nineteenth Hole by displaying one finger.

It is rather curious that, despite the fact that three of the eight cases are favorable to Mr. Prime and three are favorable to Mr. Otherwise, while only two are favorable to Mr. Square, the game is stacked in Mr. Square's favor.

(Game theorists may find it interesting to analyze the game if the restriction against coalitions is lifted.)

Word Games

45. GHOST

The game of GHOST is a well-known pastime among word lovers. The players build sequentially toward a word by adding an additional terminal letter on their turn with the objective of forcing another player to complete a word (uncapitalized, and of at least three letters). A player who adds a letter which results in a sequence with which no word begins loses a point if an opponent disputes his play.

Black has challenged you to a two-man game of GHOST. There will be only one round. In two-man GHOST most letters are traps (unsafe against best play). For instance, an opening of V is suicidal. Opponent can add Y and opener is stuck with completing the only word starting with those two letters, "Vying." On the other hand L, which appears to be an immediate trap in which the second player adds another L (with *llama* in mind), is safe, at least from that attack. First player replies with Y, and second player is stuck with *llyn* (a lake or pool).

Black draws first play. How do you respond if he opens with A? B? C? D? All of these are traps for Black.

Solution to GHOST

Against B you respond W and make a ghost out of Black with *bwana.*
Against C you respond T, winning with *ctetology.* Against D, respond
V, giving Black a choice of A or O. He then loses against *dvandva* or
dvornik. Against A, respond Y. Black has five options: A, E, L, O, and
W, losing respectively to *ayapana, ayelp, aylet, ayont,* and *aywhere.*

A very patient logophile could relegate two-man GHOST to the
completely analyzed status of TIC–TAC–TOE by determining all safe
and unsafe openings. A sufficiently difficult challenge is to find just one
safe opening letter (with which first player can win against any responses
by his opponent).

Sidegame:
We could call this THE LAST WORD in games. Two players, each
equipped with a copy of the same dictionary (any dictionary will do),
proceed as follows: first player announces any 3-letter word starting
with A. Each succeeding play is the modification of the opponent's last
word to a new word in which only one of the letters has been altered.
Also each new word must appear *later* in the dictionary. Thus AID
may be followed by AIR, AND, or RID, among others. Loser is the
first player stymied.

46. GEOGRAPHY

Remember the game of GEOGRAPHY? Each player in turn names a country starting with the final letter of the preceding country: England–Denmark–Kuwait–Tibet–Turkey–Yemen, for example, until some player is stumped or fails to meet the established time limit.

Not a very interesting game, really. It can last for hours. A more stimulating version can be played with the fifty states and with the sequence open at both ends. Thus after four plays, if the sequence has been Hawaii–Idaho–Oregon–North Dakota, the next player can either add Utah at the left or, say, Arkansas on the right.

You and Black play a two-man version of OPEN–ENDED GEOGRAPHY with states. The first player to be stumped twice loses. The rules permit a stumped player to begin the next sequence and prohibit the use of any state more than once during the entire match.

A coin flip gives Black first play and he starts with KENTUCKY, forcing you to prefix with NEW YORK. He now stumps you with, say, WASHINGTON. First round to Black and you now begin the second round. Your play.

Solution to GEOGRAPHY

There is only one state that is an immediate stumper, and you had better use it, for Black quite possibly knows it too. So even if you are lucky enough to win the second round with another state as opener, he will be apt to win the match by using it on the third round. Your only hope is that he is not so expert in the game as to know the other safe openings, such as Wyoming. If not, you stand a good chance of winning, as most of the fifty state openings are traps, losing against best play.

So you play the quick winner, MAINE, and hope for the best.

It is not difficult to determine for all fifty states which are the safe and unsafe openings; in fact, it makes an interesting pastime.

If you feel you're ready for a tougher challenge involving a three-man version of the game, see Notes and Sources.

47. SCRABBLE

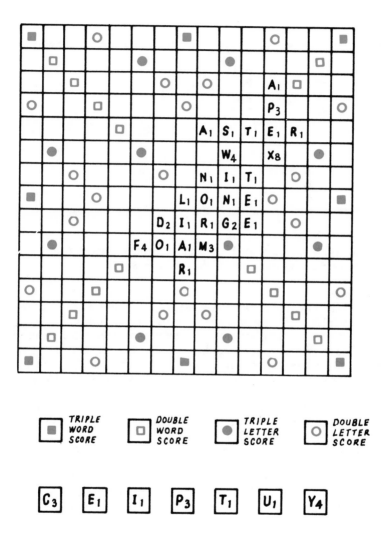

At a critical point in a SCRABBLE game you are confronted with the word arrangement shown above and the letters C, E, I, P, T, U, and Y to play with. Naturally you would like to be able to play all seven letters, though the possibility seems remote. In any event your objective is to maximize your score.

Solution to SCRABBLE

By a stroke of luck you can get rid of all seven letters, as follows:

```
          A
    P     P
    EASTER
    C  W X
    UNIT
    LONE
    DIRGE
 FOAM
    R
    I
    T
    Y
```

This will give you a total score of 72, which is more than you can hope to get by using one of the triple word scores.

Sidegame:
In the game of CRASH two players each writes down a five-letter word. Then the players fire simultaneous "salvos" at each other. A salvo is a group of five test words selected in an attempt to deduce the opponent's word. He scores each word according to the number of "crashes" (occurrences of the same letter in the *same* position) it makes with his secret word. For example, BEGIN scores two crashes against REGAL, while LARGE scores none.

In a game of CRASH your first salvo of STRAW, HOLLY, TEPID, MINUS, and COURT draws five zeroes. Your second salvo draws one crash per word: BRING, GLOVE, SHEIK, TRUCE, and FLIES. Select a salvo which will guarantee you a bullseye on your next turn.

(A little study will confirm that there are only three possible target words, *all generically related,* unless you permit the *Mad Magazine* word BLECH—a term of extreme repugnance, as applied for example to this sidegame, which many logophiles regard as a CRASHing bore!)

48. FISH SOUP

In the game of FISH SOUP nine cards bearing the words above are placed face up on a table. Alternately you and your opponent draw cards with the object of obtaining three which share a common letter. The first player (if any) to succeed in this wins.

By a flip of a coin your opponent wins the advantage of first move. He promptly takes the card marked KNIT. Your move.

Solution to **FISH SOUP**

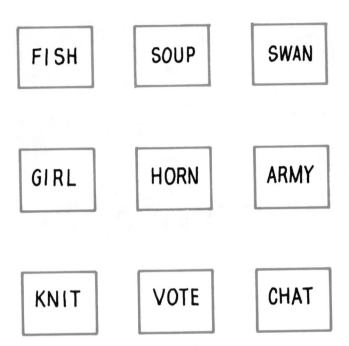

If the cards are arranged in a three-by-three array as above, FISH SOUP emerges as a disguised version of TIC–TAC–TOE. The eight rows may be characterized by the common letters: I, O, and A for the columns, S, R, and T for the rows, and H and N for the two diagonals.

Any TIC–TAC–TOE player knows that there is only one way to defend against a corner opening: by taking the center. Otherwise the first player will seize one of the adjacent corners and trap you in a "fork" on his next move.

The only card that will prevent your opponent from winning is HORN. Once you take it, best play on both parts will result in a tie. (Or, as TIC–TAC–TOE players say, a "cat's game.")

If you memorize the array and play FISH SOUP against an uninitiated opponent, however astute, you'll win at least four out of five games playing first, and probably at least half playing second. Your frustrated opponent will, of course, never win.

Countdown and Countup Games

The following group of games are traditionally described as "subtractive" games, for obvious reasons. They vary in degree of difficulty from very simple to extremely complex. In general these games consist of several piles of objects such as coins or matches, denoted "counters," and play involves the alternate removal of counters by two players. The variety of such games results both from the removal restrictions and the ultimate objective.

It is remarkable how many different games can be based on only a single pile of counters. To illustrate this point, the one-pile or "countdown" games, comprising the simplest of the subtractive family, will all employ a pile of thirteen counters. This number is just about right to allow the reader to perform his analysis with the help of some experimentation. A smaller number of counters might make such analysis trivial; larger numbers would tend to raise the "work factor" to unmanageable size.

In keeping with this choice of thirteen counters for the games immediately following, they have all been designated by the appropriate family name **TRISKIDEKAPHILIA**.

49. TRISKIDEKAPHILIA

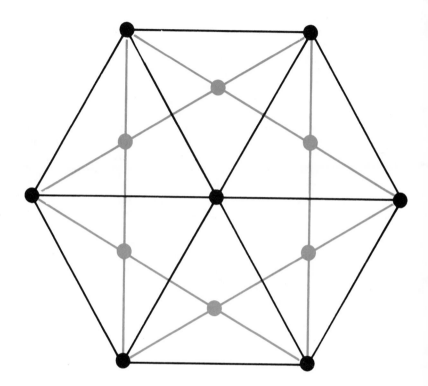

Probably the most ancient (and simplest) subtractive game involves a single "pile" of counters. The two players alternately remove one, two, up to N counters, and the winner is the player who removes the last one.

This game and the more simple one-pile games following will all be based on a pile of thirteen counters. General strategies for piles of arbitrary size will not be difficult to deduce.

In the present game, the "limit" is three; i.e., each player on his turn has the option of removing one, two, or three counters. You have first play. Your move.

Solution to **TRISKIDEKAPHILIA**

If you remove one counter, leaving twelve, you can ensure a win by responding to your opponent's moves as follows: If he takes one counter, you take three; if he takes two, you take two; if he takes three, you take one. Thus the next three exchanges of moves will each reduce the pile by four counters, and yours will be the last move.

Generalizing, let N be the limiting number of counters removable on a single play. If $N + 1$ is not a factor of the original number of counters, then the first player should remove exactly the number required to make the remainder a multiple of $N + 1$. This is the only "safe leave." The winning strategy now is to parry the removal by your opponent of K counters by removing $N + 1 - K$ counters. Thus each exchange results in the removal of $N + 1$ counters, guaranteeing you the win.

What are the winning first moves, starting with a pile of thirteen, if the option on each turn is to remove one or two counters? One, two, three, or four counters? Any number of counters from one to five? In the first case $N = 2$, making $N + 1$ a factor of 12. Remove one counter; then parry each of your opponent's moves by removing 3 minus the number removed by him. In the second case ($N = 4$), $N + 1$ is a factor of 10. Start by removing three counters, and when opponent removes K, remove $5 - K$. In the third case $N + 1 = 6$, a factor of 12. Remove one counter and parry K with $6 - K$.

Now that you have the idea, you should be able to win the game following.

50. SECOND PLAYER OPTION

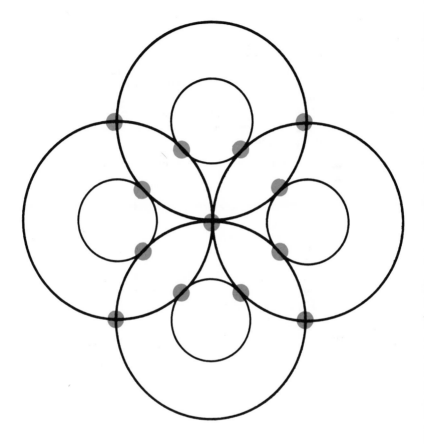

Starting again with a pile of thirteen objects, your opponent has first play. To compensate for this disadvantage you have the option of declaring the limit number N. On each move a player may remove one, two, up to N counters.

Unless you choose the right value of N, your opponent will beat you with optimal play. What N do you declare?

Solution to SECOND PLAYER OPTION

The solution to the preceding game provides the clue. Since a winning leave occurs when the number of counters left is a multiple of $N + 1$, you will, by declaring an N of 12, be effectively creating a winning leave. Whatever number of counters your opponent removes, you remove thirteen minus that number—i.e., the remainder of the counters. Twelve is the only value of N which gives you the advantage. The table below provides the winning first moves for your opponent for all other values of N, starting with a pile of thirteen counters.

LIMITING NUMBER N	WINNING FIRST MOVE
1	1
2	1
3	1
4	3
5	1
6	6
7	5
8	4
9	3
10	2
11	1
13 or more	13

51. TRISKIDEKAPHILIA MISERE

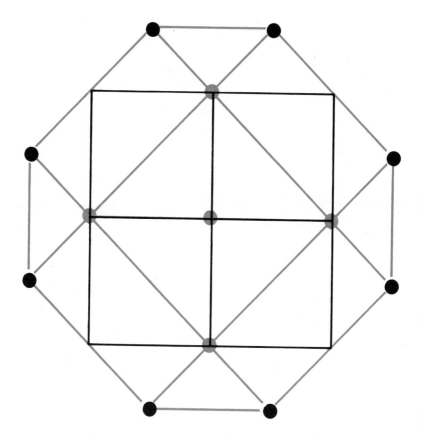

Once again there are thirteen counters. The limiting number is four, and you have first move. The objective, however, in this misere version is to force your opponent to take the last counter. You can remove one, two, three, or four. How many will it be?

Solution to **TRISKIDEKAPHILIA MISERE**

Forcing your opponent to take the last counter is equivalent to securing the next-to-last counter for yourself. So MISERE with thirteen counters is played like regular TRISKIDEKAPHILIA with twelve counters. Since $N + 1 = 5$, you play to leave a multiple of 5 (plus one additional counter). Your winning play, therefore, is to remove two counters, leaving eleven. You parry your opponent's removal of K by removing $5 - K$. Following your third move, he will be left with the losing counter.

Sidegame:
Try your hand at analyzing TRISKIDEKAPHILIA ESCALATION: First player removes 1 or 2 counters. Second player removes 1, 2, or 3. Now first player removes 1, 2, 3, or 4. And so on. Consider both the standard and misere versions.

52. RESTRICTED TRISKIDEKAPHILIA

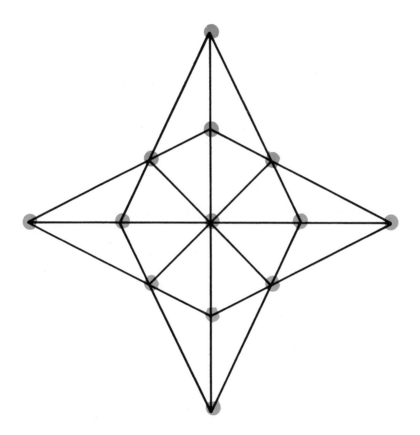

Thirteen counters, the choice of subtracting one, two, or three at every move, and you have first play.

But there is a small restriction that makes this game somewhat harder to analyze than the previous three versions. A player may not duplicate his opponent's last play. For example, if on one of his turns a player removes two counters, his opponent is required to reply either by subtracting one counter or three.

Note that one can win by

    1. removing the last counter

or 2. removing one counter at the end and leaving the other player with only one counter, thereby stymying him.

Your move.

Solution to RESTRICTED TRISKIDEKAPHILIA

Working backward, it is not difficult to establish a table of winning moves. Defining "total" as the aggregate number of counters removed after your last play, thirteen is a winning total regardless of the number of counters you remove to achieve it, and twelve is a winning total only provided you reached it by removing one counter. Eleven is always a losing total, since your opponent can win by removing either one or two counters, and not more than one of these moves is barred for him. Ten is a winning total only if you reach it by removing three, and nine, like thirteen, is always a winning total. The table given below shows how the properties of the various totals repeat in cycles of four. Note that 11, 7, and 3 are losing totals regardless of the number of counters last removed.

Winning Total Number of Counters Removed	Provided Last Play Was
13	1,2, or 3
12	1
10	3
9	1,2, or 3
8	1
6	3
5	1, 2 or 3
4	1
2	3 (impossible, of course)
1	1

The only winning opening is the removal of one counter, and the game tree illustrates your quickest winning strategy. At the end of every branch the first player either removes the last counter(s) or leaves one counter by removing one, thus depriving his opponent of a legal move.

If the first player opens with two or three, his opponent can enter the winning track by making the appropriate reply: 3 if you open with 2, and either 1 or 2 if you open with 3.

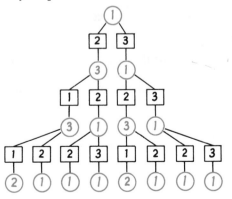

53. ODD TOTAL

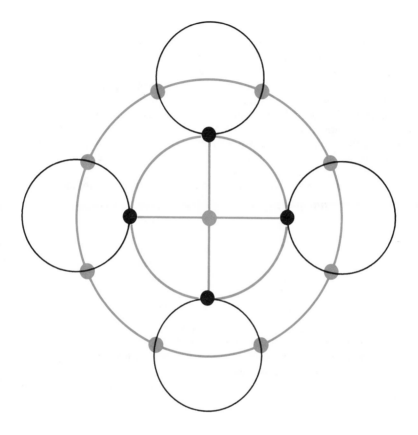

The same old pile of thirteen counters and the option of removing one, two, or three on each turn.

However, in this game you keep all the counters you remove, and the objective is to be the player who accumulates an odd number of counters.

Your opponent has first play and removes one counter. Your move.

Solution to ODD TOTAL

Again the game is solved by working backward. Zero is a winning leave (provided you have an odd total) and 1 is also. Two is always a losing leave, since your opponent can remove both if his total is odd and 1 if it is even. Three is also a losing leave, allowing your opponent to remove 2 if his total is odd or all three if it is even. Then 4 is seen to be a winning leave, but only if your total is even. In this case, you will respond to your opponent's possible play of one, two, or three counters by removing three, one, and one, respectively. On the other hand, leaving four with an odd total loses, since your opponent, whose total will be even, will remove three counters and win.

The situation is summarized by the following table of winning leaves:

Winning Leave	Provided Your Total Is
0	odd
1	odd
4	even
5	even
8	odd
9	odd
12	even

Since everything else constitutes a losing leave, the first player has the disadvantage. He cannot make a winning leave, and you may verify that whenever your opponent presents you with a losing leave, you can always convert it to a winning leave.

Your winning reply to Black's opening of one counter is to remove three.

54. ALIQUOT

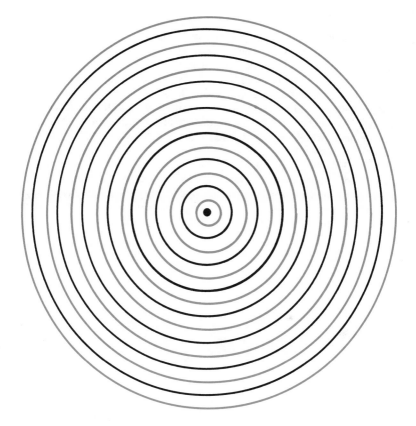

Two players start with a positive integer, and alternately subtract any aliquot part (factor) with the exception of the number itself from the number their opponent leaves. The winner is the last player able to perform such a subtraction.

For example, if the original number is 12, the first player may subtract either 1, 2, 3, 4, or 6 (but not 12). Say he subtracts 2. Then the second player is left with 10 and has the choice of subtracting 1, 2, or 5.

The objective is to leave your opponent without a move. This can be done only by leaving him a 1, since 1 is the only integer which has no aliquot part other than itself.

The starting number is 128, and you have the first play. How much do you subtract? Your choices are 1, 2, 4, 8, 16, 32, and 64.

Solution to ALIQUOT

A little analysis should have convinced you that this is really a very simple (minded?) game. The winning strategy is always to leave your opponent with an odd number. If you start with an even number, you can always do this by subtracting any odd factor. If there is no higher odd factor than 1, as is the case with 128, take away 1. Having left your opponent with an odd number, you are assured of regaining an even number on your next turn, because all factors of an odd number are odd, so that he must present you with odd minus odd, which is even. Eventually he will be left with 1.

A lazy player, faced with an even number, can simply subtract one each time, knowing that his leave is always safe. But this may give the show away, and deprive you of the opportunity of beating your opponent in a series of games. It is surprising how many games even an astute mathematician is likely to lose before he divines the secret.

55. NIM

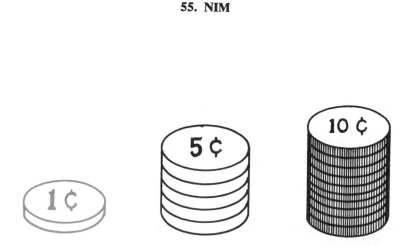

In the ancient game of NIM, the objective is to remove the last object, each play consisting of the removal from any one pile of as many objects as desired, from one to the entire pile.

You have first move at a stage in the game in which there is 1 penny, a pile of 5 nickels, and a pile of 10 dimes. You have sixteen choices: remove the penny; remove 1, 2, . . . up to all 5 nickels; or remove 1, 2, up to all 10 dimes. However, only one choice guarantees victory. Your move.

Solution to NIM

NIM has been well analyzed and generalized to any number of piles and any number of counters in each pile. The key is to partition each pile into distinct powers of two. Thus there is 1 penny, $1 + 4$ nickels, and $2 + 8$ dimes. A winning leave is created by leaving your opponent a partitioning in which no power of two appears an odd number of times. When forced to play on a winning leave, a player will always present his opponent with a losing leave, and the latter can always be converted to another winning leave.

The 8 must be eliminated, so your first play must be on the dimes. The only winning leave is created by removing 6 dimes, leaving the partions: 1, $1 + 4$, and 4.

The reader is invited to follow the game through to its conclusion, supplying Red's response to each of Black's subsequent moves. (The game ends quickly.) He is also challenged to determine Black's winning responses to Red's initial play, had he chosen any of the fifteen alternatives to removing exactly 6 dimes.

56. TSYANSHIDZI

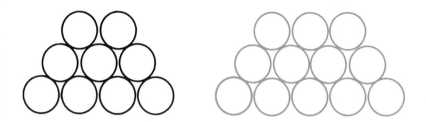

This is an ancient Chinese game, reinvented by W. A. Wythoff around the time of World War I. Two players start with two piles of chips. Alternately, each player removes chips with the option of removing

(1) any number of chips from one pile

or (2) the *same* number of chips from each pile.

As Red you have first play on piles of nine and twelve counters respectively. The advantage is yours if you make the one correct play. Otherwise, Black, who is experienced at the game, will beat you. The objective is to remove the last chip or chips.

Solution to TSYANSHIDZI

Working backward, one can generate a table of winning leaves:

(1,2)
(3,5)
(4,7)
(6,10)
(8,13)
(9,15)
(11,18)
(12,20)
(14,23)
(16,26)
etc.

The first member of each pair is the smallest positive integer that does not appear in a previous winning leave. To obtain the second member, follow the rule that the difference between the two members is always one more than that for the previous winning leave.

So the game is actually rather simple to analyze. There is even a formula for the *n*th winning leave (see Notes and Sources), which is based on the well-known Fibonacci ratio.

In the game under consideration, the correct play is to subtract five chips from each pile, leaving the winning pair (4,7).

Just for diversion, see how quickly you can determine the three alternative winning plays when confronted with piles of fifteen and twenty chips.

57. LASKER'S NIM

Emanuel Lasker, a chess immortal, concocted his own version of NIM. The objective is still to take the last counter, but a player has two options on each move. He may either reduce the size of one pile as in standard NIM, or he may divide any pile containing more than one object into two (not necessarily equal) piles.

Once again you have first play on three piles, consisting of one, five, and ten objects.

Solution to LASKER'S NIM

The general strategy for this game has also been determined (see Notes and Sources). A position is a winning leave if and only if it becomes a winning leave in standard NIM after increasing by one each pile number with remainder of 3 (modulo 4) and decreasing by one each non-zero pile number evenly divisible by 4. Since none of the pile numbers is of either form (1, 5, 10) in LASKER'S NIM corresponds to (1, 5, 10) in NIM—a losing leave, hence convertible to a winning one.

You have exactly twenty-three different plays to choose from, and only one turns out to be a winner. Examine them all. (1, 4, 10) corresponds to (1, 3, 10) in NIM, a losing leave. (1, 5, 3, 7) corresponds to (1, 5, 4, 8), another loser. The only winning leave is found to be (1, 5, 3), which corresponds to the winning leave of (1, 5, 4) in NIM.

If you are not motivated to verify that all other plays are losers, at least follow the game from (1, 5, 3) to its winning conclusion. Black has twelve options, all hopeless.

You might also consider this modification: a player may either reduce the size of one pile as in standard NIM, or he may *combine* any two piles into a single pile. What are the winning positions?

58. SHANNON'S NIM

In Claude E. Shannon's variation of NIM, a restriction is added that the number of objects removed be prime (counting one as a prime). One might expect this restriction to add a level of complexity to the analysis, but that is not the case.

Again you have first play on piles of one, five, and ten objects respectively.

Solution to SHANNON'S NIM

It is not difficult to prove that since 1, 2, and 3 are allowable removal numbers, a winning leave is one in which the pile remainders after division by 4 constitute a winning leave in standard NIM.

Since 1, 5, and 10 have respective remainders of 1, 1, and 2 (modulo 4), there are two winning openings. Either remove two strawberries, leaving remainder numbers of 1, 3, and 2, or remove two cherries, leaving remainder numbers of 1, 1, and 0, both of which are winning NIM leaves.

Open Question 1: If Shannon's restriction that only prime numbers can be removed is replaced by the restriction that only squares can be removed, what constitutes a winning leave?

Open Question 2: If SHANNON'S NIM is modified only in excluding one as a prime, what constitutes a winning leave?

59. KAYLES

The ten bowling pins are set up in a straight line. You and Black alternately roll a bowling ball at them, and the winner is the man who knocks down the last pin.

The pins are spaced in such a way that the ball can either knock down a single pin or two adjacent pins. Black, who had first roll, was confident of beating you. By aiming for the 5 and 6 pins, he would have left you with two groups of four pins and could have followed the symmetric strategy of replying on one group exactly as you played the other.

Black unfortunately hooked badly on his first roll, knocking down the 3 and 4 pins and leaving you with groups of two and six.

Assume that all future rolls will be accurate and that each player in turn must knock down at least one pin. What pin or pins should you knock over?

Solution to KAYLES

As the result of comparatively recent investigations, the game of KAYLES has been completely analyzed, using the tool of the Grundy Function. All pile numbers have Grundy numbers as indicated:

Grundy Number	1		2		3	4		5	6	7	8
	1	44	2	46	3	5	41	28	11	15	27
	4	49	7	50	6	9	48		22	23	33
	8	52	10	55	18	12	53		34	30	45
	13	56	14	58	39	17	57		70	35	51
	16	61	19	62		21	60			42	63
	20	64	26	67		24	65			47	69
	25	68	31	74		29	72			54	75
	32	73	38	79		36	77			59	81
	37	76	43	82						66	
	40	80								71	
										78	
										83	

For $N > 70$, the Grundy number of N, $g(N)$, is equal to $g(N + 12)$. A set of piles in KAYLES is a winning leave if and only if the Grundy numbers of the piles constitute a winning leave in NIM. Thus the only winning play is for Red to knock down either the 6 and 7 pins or the 8 and 9 pins, in either case, leaving piles of 1, 2, and 3 (with Grundy numbers 1, 2, and 3). It is a simple task to show that any other leave by Red is a loser, even without resort to the Grundy Table.

The structure of KAYLES is still rather mystifying. Only one number has a Grundy number of 5. And since all numbers greater than 70 have Grundy numbers of either 1, 2, 4, 7, or 8, we have among other surprising conclusions the fact that *any* three piles of more than 70 objects constitute a losing leave in KAYLES.

60. GRUNDY'S GAME

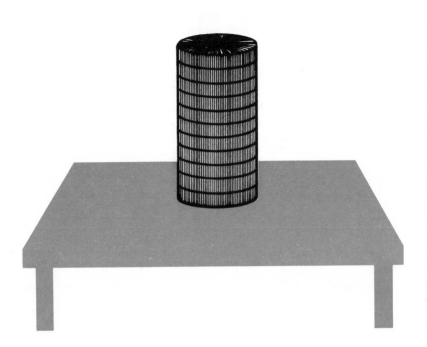

Grundy's Game, modestly named DISTICH by its inventor, is a two-player game played with any number of piles having assorted numbers of counters.

The players move alternately, each play consisting of dividing any pile into two *unequal* piles. Thus a pile of 4 can be converted into piles of 3 and 1, while a pile of 1 or 2 is unplayable.

The winner is the last player able to make a legal move.

Starting with a single pile of 11 counters, you are permitted to make the first play.

Solution to GRUNDY'S GAME

This is a tough one. Unless you know how to compute Grundy Functions, you must resort to the game-tree approach and the process of elimination. (Eleven is just small enough to make the work factor reasonable.)

Were you familiar with the Grundy Function technique (see Notes and Sources), you would obtain the following table for DISTICH:

Pile Size (N)	Grundy Number $g(N)$
1	0
2	0
3	1
4	0
5	2
6	1
7	0
8	2
9	1
10	0
11	2

You could then quickly conclude that there are two winning plays: (1,10) and (4,7), both corresponding to the winning NIM leave of (0,0). The three alternative plays (2,9), (3,8), and (5,6) are all losers. They can all be converted by your opponent to (2,3,6), corresponding to the winning NIM leave of (0,1,1).

61. SUBTRACT–A–SQUARE

Starting with 42 counters, you and your opponent alternately remove any number of counters from those remaining with the proviso that the number removed at each turn be a perfect square. As first player, you have the choice of removing 1, 4, 9, 16, 25, or 36 counters. How many do you remove? Winner is the player who removes the last counter.

Solution to SUBTRACT–A–SQUARE

Clearly a player with one counter left will win; with two he will lose. Working backward, it is easy to generate a table of winning and losing leaves:

Winning Leaves	Losing Leaves		
2	1	19	32
5	3	21	33
7	4	23	35
10	6	24	36
12	8	25	37
15	9	26	38
17	11	27	40
20	13	28	41
22	14	29	42
34	16	30	
39	18	31	

The only way to obtain a winning leave is to remove 25 counters.

This "backward" technique will prove useful in the "additive" games that follow.

144

62. THE LAST PRIME (A Five-Finger Exercise)

Two players alternately hold up any number of fingers from one to five. The cumulative total is kept and the object is to keep the total prime. The first player who is unable to raise the total to a higher prime is the loser. You draw the first move. How many fingers do you hold up?

Solution to A FIVE–FINGER EXERCISE

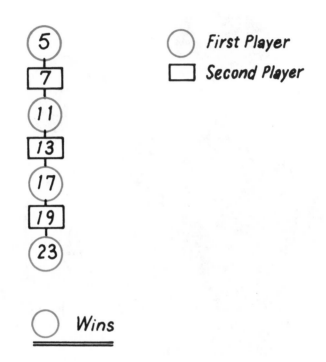

The objective is to be the player who first reaches a total that is a prime at least 6 less than the next higher prime. Then the opponent will be stymied.

The first such prime is 23. Since you wish to arrive at this total, you want your opponent to arrive at a total of 19. Reasoning backward, the desired sequence is 23, 19, 17, 13, 11, 7, and 5, with your totals in red.

Thus your first play should be five fingers.

The game tree shown above lists the totals at each play. The tree is simple, consisting of a single branch; this indicates that at each turn the second player's move is forced.

146

63. THE LAST PRIME (Two-Hand Version)

This game is a variation of the preceding game; the only difference is that the number of fingers allowed is from one to ten. Again, you are the first player. How many fingers do you hold up?

Solution to TWO–HAND VERSION

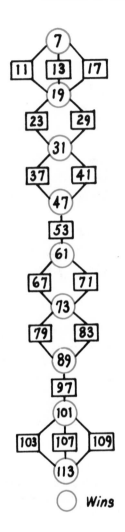

⚪ *First Player*
⬜ *Second Player*

⚪ *Wins*

The first gap of ten or more between successive primes occurs with the pair 113, 127. Thus 113 is the goal you should aim for. 113 can be reached in one move from 103, 107, or 109, but not from 101. Hence 101 is your subgoal. Moving backward methodically, you will arrive at the game tree depicted above, in which your first play must be 7.

You should have little trouble applying the "backward" technique to the one- and two-hand versions of THE LAST SQUARE.

64. HYBRID

Now that you know the general procedure for computing winning strategies in games such as THE LAST PRIME and THE LAST SQUARE, you should be able to apply it to the game of HYBRID. You have first move, and each player in turn raises the total by any number from one to ten with the requirement that the new total be *either* prime or square. Winner is the last player able to make a legal move.

You have seven options for your first play: 1, 2, 3, 4, 5, 7, or 9. Only one of them guarantees you a win against opponent's best play.

Solution to HYBRID

199 is the objective, being the smallest number out of reach of either a square or a prime. The next square is 225, the next prime 211. Working backward, the winning opening is found to be 2. Any of the other six openings permits your opponent to move into the "winning track."

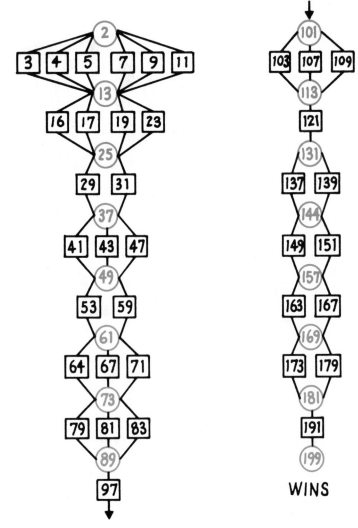

WINS

65. OPTION

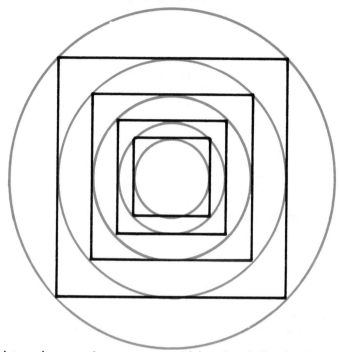

An interesting two-player game, combining the challenging features of the purely additive and purely subtractive games, with rather perplexing consequences.

A positive integer is selected, and the players alternately modify it by exercising one of two options: either add to or subtract from the present number the largest square that does not exceed it. The winner is the first player to leave a zero.

Some examples will be of interest. Eleven is a losing leave, since your opponent can convert it to 20. You are now faced with the dilemma of giving your opponent either 4 or 36, both of which present him with an immediate win.

Five is a winning leave since your opponent must present you either with 1 or 9. What about 3? Your opponent must convert it to 2 (avoiding 4) and you must convert the 2 back to a 3 (avoiding 1). Hence 3 is clearly a tying leave. It follows that 7 is also a tying leave. It must be converted to the tying leave 3 in order to avoid 11, which has already been shown to be a losing leave.

With these preliminaries you are ready to play OPTION. You have first play. What is your move if the original number is 52? How about 48?

Solution to OPTION

Working purely by hand, starting with small numbers and working up, it is not difficult (indeed it is an amusing pastime) to determine winning, losing, and tying positions. Among the integers from 1 to 138, only 8 are winning leaves, namely 5, 20, 29, 45, 80, 101, 116, and 135. Twenty-seven are losing leaves: 1, 4, 9, 11, 14, 16, 21, 25, 30, 36, 41, 44, 49, 52, 54, 64, 69, 71, 81, 84, 86, 100, 105, 120, 121, 126, and 136. All the remaining 103 numbers are tying leaves.

Since 52 is a losing leave, you should win if confronted with it. But you must not subtract 49, since that will present your opponent with the tying leave 3. Add 49, leaving your opponent 101. He cannot afford to subtract 100 so must give you back 201, from which you subtract 196, presenting him with the winning leave 5. You will obtain a zero on your next turn, playing either 1 or 9.

But if the starting number is 48, the best you can hope for against optimum play is a tie. Caution is required. If you add 36, presenting your opponent with 84, he will convert it to 165, a winning leave. You are forced either to reply with 21 or 309. In the first case, he will leave you a 5 and beat you. In the second, he will convert to 20, also a winning leave. Therefore you must subtract 36, leaving 12. Now your opponent cannot afford to leave 21 and is forced to convert to the tying number 3.

There seems little rhyme or reason to the sequence of winning, losing, and tying leaves, though the generating principle is explicit and simple. Readers are challenged to develop a formula for winning leaves in the game of OPTION.

"Life Games"

66. CAVE CANEM

Driving in unfamiliar territory, you stop to get directions at a large house with a fenced-in front lawn. Absent-mindedly you neglect a sign at the gate which says BEWARE OF DOG. You are halfway to the house when you suddenly see a vicious-looking Doberman Pinscher streaking toward you with teeth bared. You have neither a weapon nor protective clothing such as a jacket with which to defend yourself. And you haven't a chance of getting back to the gate in time. Your move!

153

Solution to CAVE CANEM

Those familiar with the canine species know that the universal signal of submission is the assumption of a supine position. Dogs instinctively refrain from attacking a foe who has surrendered, so your best chance is to lie on your back with arms and legs upward like a puppy who is getting the worst of a fight and wishes to call it off.

If you are lucky and the Doberman has only the natural viciousness of his breed, he will sniff you thoroughly and possibly "guard" you, in which case you must remain motionless and wait patiently for the owner to appear.

If, however, the dog has received special watchdog training, there is a possibility that he may not yield to his instinct to honor your "surrender." If he attacks, you must protect your throat with your forearms, while lashing out with both feet in what you hope will be a well-timed kick. If you once achieve the initiative, you will then attempt, even at the cost of severe bites, to grab one of his hind legs, a dog's weak spot. If by twisting it inward you succeed in breaking it, the Doberman will have lost his attack potential. You will, of course, be required to reimburse the owner for injuries to the dog and will have to pay the costs for your own. But you will probably have saved your life.

Next time, pay attention to signs.

67. BLIND CURVE

Driving along a freeway on a weekday afternoon you find that your car has lost all power. Could be a clogged fuel pump or perhaps a broken battery cable or any one of 1001 other ills that cars are heir to. By the time you have convinced yourself that the car is really out of action, it has decelerated considerably. You head for the right-hand shoulder, but your momentum is insufficient, and you coast to a stop in a diagonal position straddling the rightmost dividing line, thereby blocking the two right lanes.

The traffic has been sparse and that is a blessing, but by mischance your car has come to rest in the worst possible spot: the end of a curve in the freeway. Ordinarily, visibility is sufficient, even on freeway curves, for oncoming drivers to take corrective action. The problem in this case is that alongside the freeway is a mountain which obscures your car from view. The imminent danger is not to you, since you can step out onto the shoulder. Nor are you worried so much about the danger to your car. Steel is replaceable. But human lives are at stake, many of them. Barring the possibility of superhuman reflexes on the part of the drivers due to approach the curve in the two rightmost lanes, there is an ominous threat of multiple collisions.

The car is too heavy for you to push singlehandedly. You have no flares or emergency beacons. There is no time to waste regretting that you didn't head for the shoulder when you still had enough momentum to get you there. Your move.

Solution to BLIND CURVE

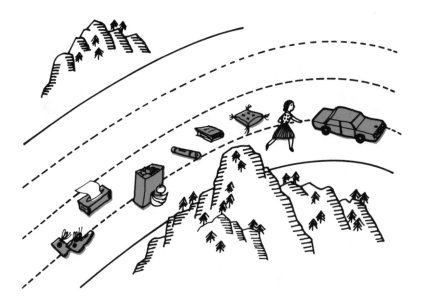

Grab everything movable that you can carry—purse, cushions, road maps, packages, etc., and sprint back along the shoulder to the point where the curve begins. If a car is approaching in one of the right-hand lanes, signal him to slow down. If he is far enough away, you will have time to signal more emphatically by strewing your armful of objects over the two lanes.

During your return to the car add to the litter by throwing whatever large rocks you can find into the danger lanes. When you get back to the car, you will seize another armful for reinforcement of your danger signal, though you have probably succeeded in averting a collision already. Just to make certain, you will continue to strew the highway until you have assured yourself that even the most oblivious driver will vacate the right lanes in time to escape injury. If you run out of movable objects, don't forget your shoes and other articles of clothing.

Possibly this is the only case in which the highway patrol will compliment you for littering the highway.

68. RUNAWAY

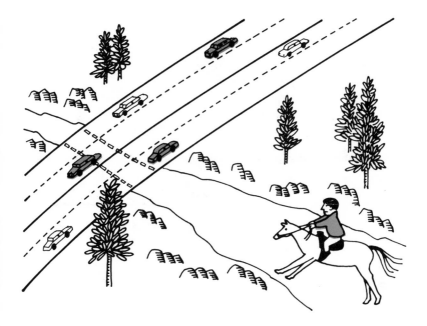

You are riding a spirited horse along a level trail. Suddenly the horse is "spooked" (for reasons known only to the horse). Stretching his neck forward, he begins galloping at top speed as if he were coming from behind in a stakes race. Knowing that little more than half a mile ahead the trail is intersected by a busy highway, you realize the danger is acute. You try "pumping" the reins, alternately tightening and slackening them; the frightened horse merely gallops faster. You try heading him toward the side, but he has the bit in his teeth and will not be turned.

You consider "ejecting," but even apart from the sharp rocks lining both sides of the trail, you are well aware that you would be fortunate to escape severe fractures if you jumped off at such high speed. The presence of the rocks increases the risk of fatal head injury. You are now about 300 yards from the highway crossing and can see cars passing rapidly in both directions. Your move!

Solution to RUNAWAY

Place the reins over the pommel, whip off your jacket, and with a sleeve in each hand, drape it over the horse's head. A "blind" horse invariably stops, but the danger is not over. While decelerating, the horse is likely to stumble and fall. To prevent this you secure both sleeves of the jacket with one hand, regain the reins with the other, and with gentle pressure keep the horse to the center of the trail until he comes to a full stop.

Any attempt to cover the horse's eyes with your hands is doomed to failure unless you are built like a chimpanzee, since the horse can counter by extending his neck forward and down. This I can guarantee from experience.

69. DANGER ACUTE

You have borrowed your friend's desert cabin for a solitary vacation during which you plan to augment your rock and mineral collection and catch up on your reading.

The first night you are troubled by nausea and stomach cramps and retire early, hoping that whatever it is will have gone away by the time you awaken.

At 5 A.M. your sleep is interrupted by severe abdominal pains which start at your left side but gradually radiate toward the right—the unmistakable signs of acute appendicitis.

Almost thoroughly incapacitated, the idea of driving back to civilization over 55 miles of unbelievably bad dirt road in a jeep is ruled out. Your friend has equipped the cabin with a telephone but has, unfortunately, discontinued service on it.

Since this is flat desert country with sparse vegetation, you know that there are no ranger stations which could be alerted by a signal fire.

Alone and 55 miles from help, your situation is desperate. Nevertheless, the means are available for saving your life. Your move.

Solution to DANGER ACUTE

Though the telephone is disconnected, it is the key to the dilemma. For in rural country, where there are telephones, there are telephone lines.

If ice is available, the application of it to the painful area will be a helpful measure. But the summoning of help is the priority action. The dilemma on which this problem is based actually occurred. In the words of the protagonist:

> I drove to the nearest telephone pole, siphoned some gasoline from the jeep and saturated the pole with it as high as I could reach, and ignited it. The pole burned nicely and in a few minutes the upper part toppled, severing all four cables. Then I limped back to the cabin, applied ice to my side, and waited for the line crew to appear. They came in two and a half hours, and when I explained my reason for committing arson, they drove me at top speed to the nearest hospital, alerting them on the way by radiotelephone to be ready for an emergency appendectomy. . . . Things turned out well, and when I was able to walk after the operation, they not only gave me a free ride back to the cabin, but the company flatly refused my offer to compensate them for the damage. . . .

Telephone cables consist of wire bundles handling thousands of connections, and it is not surprising that line crews react quickly, easily locating break points by measuring the resistance in the grounded lines.

Potpourri II

70. THE MAN ON FIRST

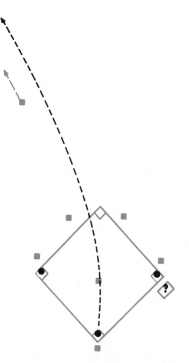

You're the first-base coach for the visiting team in a Major League baseball game. The setting: Your team is behind one run in the top of the ninth inning. You have men on first and third with one out. The batter lofts a long fly ball toward deep left field, and it looks like an even-money proposition whether the left fielder will be able to get there in time to catch it.

The runner on third "tags up," of course, as he will have plenty of time to cross home plate with the tying run if the ball is caught, even against the left fielder's strong arm. Your problem, however, is to instruct the runner on first base. You will order him either to run hard, hoping that the fly will not be caught, in which case he is virtually sure of scoring the potential winning run, or to take a waiting position between first and second base, which will enable him to get back to first base, avoiding the double play should the fly be caught.

A tough decision, but one you must, in your capacity as first-base coach, make instantly.

Solution to THE MAN ON FIRST

Those unfamiliar with the rules of baseball are apt to think the problem much easier than it actually is. They will order the runner at first base to play it safe in order to "protect" the tying run against the possible double play. The runner on third, however, needs no protection. If the fly is caught, the throw to first base is nearly as far as the throw to home plate, so that the runner on third will cross the plate before the double play is completed. In a fly-ball double play, unlike a force double play, the run will score, so the tying run is safe in any event. This reduces the problem to optimizing the chance of putting across the potential winning run.

If the fly ball is caught, you'll go into the bottom of the ninth inning with the score tied if you instruct the runner to move, while if you order him to play it safe, you'll still be in the top of the ninth with two outs, a tie score, and a man on first. An improvement, but only a negligible one. With two outs the odds are very much against scoring a runner on first.

If the left fielder is unable to reach the ball in time, you will score the potential winning run if the runner on first is instructed to move, while if he plays it safe, he is most likely to end up on third with one out. In the latter case, he has many chances of scoring, including a long fly by the next batter, a tough infield play, an error, or a passed ball. But these chances by no means add up to certainty.

Going into the bottom of the ninth with a tie score, the pressure on the visiting team is severe. If instead, the visiting team is ahead, the pressure is transferred to the home team. Most managers would favor the "bird in hand" philosophy and would prefer their coaches to order the man on first to run. If the fly is not caught, the go-ahead run is a practical certainty, while if the fly is caught, the play-it-safe strategy buys little.

In short: instruct that man on first to run for home.

71. THE PRESSURE COOKER

As coach of a college football team, your side is ahead 9 to 7 with five minutes left in the fourth quarter, your reliable place-kicker having scored a field goal in each of the first three quarters.

On a perfectly executed option play, your quarterback throws a strike to his receiver in the end zone, putting you ahead 15 to 7. The other team has earned a reputation for coming from behind, and with no time-outs used up, they have ample time to score a touchdown and a field goal (or even two touchdowns).

Do you go for the one-point conversion or try for the two-point conversion by a run or pass play?

Solution to THE PRESSURE COOKER

Scoring the two-point conversion may save the game, even if your opponents are able to score a touchdown and a field goal in the last five minutes. If *they* play it safe by attempting the one-point conversion, you will at least tie and will win if they miss. Should they "go for broke," you will win or lose, depending on whether or not they score the two-pointer.

But all this is gloomy speculation, not best calculated to win hard-fought college football games. Your objective should not be to prepare yourself to cope with the possibility that they may score a field goal and a touchdown, but to place them under the burden of having to do so. You will fail in this objective if the two-pointer is unsuccessful. Send in that reliable place-kicker and settle for the one-pointer. If he makes it you will have a nine-point cushion which will make you "touchdown-proof." This will place your opponents in the "pressure cooker."

72. FIFTEEN

In turn, you and Black pick up one of the above cards. The winner is the first player, if any, to accumulate *three* cards whose total is fifteen.

The ace counts as one only. What is your first move?

Suppose the ace is allowed to count either as one or ten? What would your strategy be?

Solution to FIFTEEN

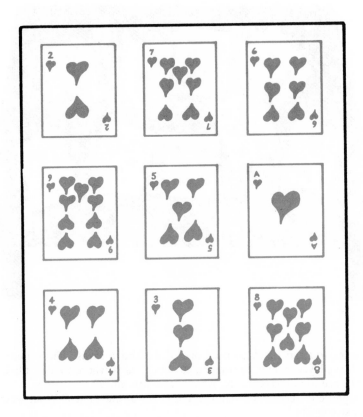

Once again, as in FISH SOUP, we have a disguised version of TIC–TAC–TOE. By placing the cards in a magic square, we observe that the three row, three column, and two diagonal totals are the only possible fifteens obtainable as the total of three cards. Hence against best play the game is a tie in the standard version, and unless Black is uninitiated, one move is as good as another.

In the alternate version in which ace counts either one or ten, ace-deuce-trey constitutes another triple which totals fifteen. You can win easily by opening with either the ace or the trey.

73. TEN OR TWENTY

The procedure is the same as in fifteen, but the goal is to obtain three cards whose total is either ten or twenty. Ace counts as one only.

The structure of this game is quite different from the TIC–TAC–TOE model of FIFTEEN. Given unrestricted choice, the first player has an easy win. Suppose Black has first play, but you have the privilege of stipulating his initial selection. What card will you require him to pick?

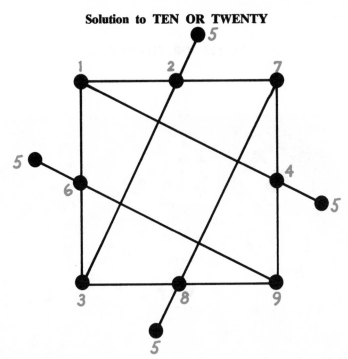

Geometrically, the game has the structure shown above, in which any three numbers in a straight line constitute a win. Since, with respect to 5, the remaining odd numbers and the evens are arranged symmetrically, the analysis is simple.

Against a 5 opening, if the response is odd, say 1, then 7 forces 8, and 9 wins. If the response is even, say 2, then 4 forces 1, and 7 wins. In the first case the third move poses the double threat 4, 6; in the second the double threat is 8, 9.

Against an odd opening, say 1, there are five possible responses, considering symmetry:

Opening	Response	Continuation
1	5	3-6-9-8-7 wins
1	2	5-4-6 wins
1	3	5-4-7 wins
1	4	7-2-5-8-6 wins
1	9	5-4-7 wins

The final moves create the respective double threats: 2, 4; 3, 9; 2, 8; 3, 9; and 2, 8. Thus by symmetry all five odd openings are winners. Therefore, you should restrict Black to any even-numbered opening, after which you will take the 5. At best, Black can tie; and, if he is not cautious, he will lose. If you were forced to open 2 and your opponent responded 5, what would your next move be?

74. RUSSIAN ROULETTE (Modified)

In this harmless version of Russian Roulette two players alternately shoot a six-shot revolver, only one chamber of which contains a cartridge, at a target. The player who first gets a "bang" rather than a "click" is the loser.

There is an option however. At any turn, instead of shooting the next chamber, a player may randomly spin the magazine before shooting. Once either player elects to spin before shooting, all successive shots, if any, must be preceded by a spin.

You have first shot. Do you spin first and shoot, or shoot without spinning?

After you have worked this one out, decide what you would do as the first player in the misere version (first player to get a "bang" wins).

Solution to RUSSIAN ROULETTE

Let P be the probability of winning for the first player who spins. In one out of six cases, he loses immediately. In the other five, the other player will have the same probability P of winning. Thus $P = \frac{5}{6}(1 - P)$ and $P = \frac{5}{11}$. Now let N be the number of chambers remaining, assuming neither player has yet exercised the spin option. The chance of winning is no better than $\frac{N-1}{N}(1 - P)$ if no spin is made, and this chance is always less than $\frac{5}{11}$ except when N = 6, in which case it is equal to $\frac{5}{11}$. (Obviously spinning prior to the first shot does not affect the first player's odds, provided his opponent plans to spin on his turn.)

It follows that after the first shot, it is always desirable to spin, and that prior to the first shot it apparently makes no difference. Ah, but it does make a difference! For if you elect not to spin and get a "click," your opponent, who may not have worked out the game, is liable not to spin either, in which case (provided he also gets a "click") you will spin prior to the third shot. By not spinning you offer him the opportunity of foolishly lowering his odds by 4 per cent. Had you spun prior to the first shot, he would have had no opportunity of making a mistake, and would be compelled to adopt the best strategy.

So your best chance is obtained by not spinning prior to the first shot, and spinning on all successive shots.

In the misere version, analysis is more difficult. Working backward, on the fifth shot, spinning gives odds of $\frac{6}{11}$ against $\frac{1}{2}$ without spinning. So spinning is superior at shot five. At shot four, spinning gives odds of $\frac{6}{11}$ against $\frac{1}{3} + \frac{2}{3} \times \frac{5}{11}$ or $\frac{7}{11}$ without spinning, so that no spinning is superior. At shot three, no spinning gives odds of $\frac{1}{4} + \frac{3}{4} \times \frac{4}{11}$ or $\frac{23}{44}$ and spinning is superior. At shot two, no spinning gives odds of $\frac{1}{5} + \frac{4}{5} \times \frac{5}{11} = \frac{31}{55}$, making no spinning the better percentage play. It follows that the first player should deny his opponent the opportunity of electing not to spin and should spin prior to his first shot, giving himself maximum odds of $\frac{6}{11}$.

75. RENCONTRE

The equipment in this two-man game is a rack with thirteen spaces and the thirteen diamonds from a pack of playing cards. The objective of the player designated the "matcher" is to place the cards in their appropriate slots (as in the illustration). The first play consists of a random shuffling of the cards, with both players having the option of cuts and recuts in order to insure the integrity of the shuffle. The matcher now places the cards in the empty spaces from left to right, hoping for as many "matches" as possible. A typical match would be the placement of the deuce in the second slot. Following each play, all correctly matched cards are left in their slots, and the next play resembles the first, except that only the unmatched cards are shuffled and laid out from left to right in the vacant slots.

When all thirteen cards have been correctly placed, the matcher receives $10 from the other player, designated the "banker." The banker, who plays a passive role throughout the game except for participating in the shuffles whenever he chooses, hopes that the matcher will require a large number of plays to achieve the final match, since the matcher must pay the banker $1 before each round.

There is, of course, no strategy at all to this game. It is purely probabilistic. Suppose your opponent offers you the choice of being banker or matcher. Which role would you choose?

Solution to RENCONTRE

Suppose there are three cards instead of thirteen. There are six equally probable arrangements on the first play:

$$
\begin{array}{lll}
1\ 2\ 3 & (3\ \text{matches}) \\
1\ 3\ 2 & (1\ \text{match}) \\
2\ 1\ 3 & (1\ \text{match}) \\
2\ 3\ 1 & (\text{no match}) \\
3\ 1\ 2 & (\text{no match}) \\
3\ 2\ 1 & (1\ \text{match})
\end{array}
$$

The expected number of matches is $\frac{1}{6}\ (3) + \frac{3}{6}\ (1) + \frac{2}{6}\ (0) = 1$.

It is simple to generalize to the case of N cards. The probability that a given card is matched in its correct position is $1/N$, and since there are N cards, the expected number of matches is N times $1/N$ or 1. Thus for any number of cards, the expected number of matches per play is one. Though this fact is perhaps difficult to accept, it can easily be verified by experiment.

Now if one match is expected on each play, N plays are expected to achieve the final match. With thirteen cards at a dollar a play, the fair payoff by the banker is exactly $13.

Since the payoff has been established as $10, the banker has a positive expectation, in this case, of $3. Let your opponent be the matcher.

76. PLAN YOUR MOVE(S), KID!

P	*L*	*A*	*N*
Y	*O*	*U*	*R*
M	*O*	*V*	*E,*
K	**D!**	*I*	

In this solitaire game, the letters are to be thought of as engraved on tiles, which are free to slide vertically or horizontally into the vacant space.

By judiciously manipulating that vacant space, you are challenged to ungarble the message as it appears above, so that it will spell out the intended message, PLAN YOUR MOVE, KID!

You can play this game by cutting out fifteen cardboard squares, lettered appropriately, and pushing them around a 4-by-4 diagram. There is no time limit.

Solution to PLAN YOUR MOVE(S), KID!

Those familiar with Sam Loyd's celebrated Fifteen Puzzle, in which the solver is challenged to manipulate the numbers in the array

```
 1  2  3  4
 5  6  7  8
 9 10 11 12
13 15 14
```

until they have been placed in proper numerical sequence, may have quickly concluded that the PLAN YOUR MOVE, KID! arrangement is impossible to attain. The Fifteen Puzzle has been proven impossible to solve, based on the fact that regardless of the number of manipulations, the number of "exchanges" performed is always even.

On the other hand, those unfamiliar with the impossibility of the Fifteen Puzzle are likely, after patient manipulation, to have ungarbled the PLAN YOUR MOVE, KID! puzzle successfully. How can this be?

The puzzles are different. The difference is in the fact that the letter O appears twice. Thus an even number of exchanges can be effected by interchanging the two Os as well as the D and the I. If the reader begins by interchanging the Os as quickly as possible, he will find that the ungarbled message rapidly falls into place.

This is one of many instances in which the less knowledge the solver is burdened with, the more apt he is to find the solution.

77. A WAR GAME

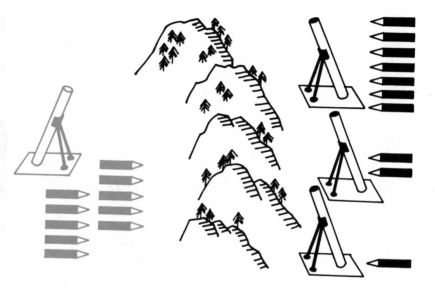

This is a problem in weapon allocation. Imagine that you have a mortar set up with ten shells and that you are ready to fire them in sequence. Within your range are three enemy mortars, A, B, and C, which your intelligence unit has determined to have respectively, seven, two, and one shell. None of them is ready to fire, and you have time to get off all your shells before they have a chance to retaliate.

You are within range of each of the three enemy mortars, no two of which are close enough to be destroyed by a single shot. Your problem is complicated by the fact that although you know the coordinates of A, B, and C, your view of them is obstructed by the terrain. In other words, you have no damage-assessment capability which would enable you to stop wasting shells on a dead mortar and concentrate on the live ones.

Obviously in minimizing the expected retaliatory capability of the three mortars, priority should be given to A over B and B over C. The question is how many of your ten shells should be allocated to each mortar? Assume that every time you fire you have a probability of $\frac{1}{2}$ of hitting your target.

Solution to WAR GAME

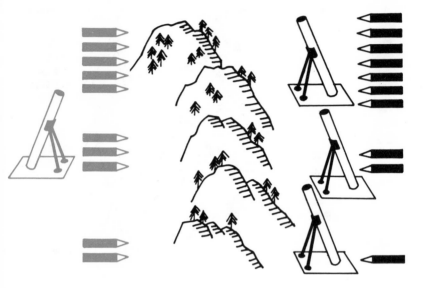

Though I have seen problems of this nature programmed for solution by digital computers, the solution by hand is very simple. It is based on the expected number of mortar shells at A, B, and C following each of your shots.

Originally A, B, and C have 7, 2, and 1 shell, denoted (7,2,1). Since A is the greatest threat, your first shot should be against it. Since your "kill probability" is $\frac{1}{2}$, the expected number of shells becomes (3.5, 2, 1). A is still the greatest threat, so you fire the second shot at A also, reducing the expected enemy arsenal to (1.75, 2, 1). Now B is the greatest threat and is, therefore, the recipient of the third shot, which produces the expected threat (1.75, 1, 1).

Continuing in this fashion, the fourth shot is directed against A, the fifth and sixth against B and C, the seventh against A, the eighth and ninth against B and C, and the tenth against A. Recapitulating, A received 5 shots, B:3, and C:2. Many intuitively feel that the optimal allocation should be proportional to the size of the enemy arsenals, and would direct 7, 2, and 1 shots against A, B and C, respectively. However, proportional assignment is generally not optimal. The optimal allocation is heavily dependent on your kill probability (though independent of that of the enemy).

176

78. THE SPIDER AND THE FLY

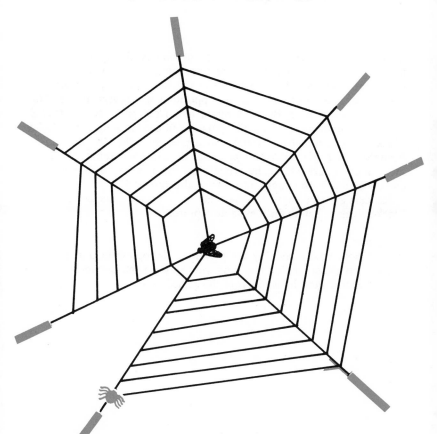

Black, the fly, is at the center of the web. You, in the role of the Red SPIDER, are at the bottom left. Your objective is to capture Black; his, to avoid capture. You have first move. Each move consists of traveling to an adjacent intersection. Moves are made alternately, and the Red strands of the web are off limits to both players. Thus both players are confined to the web, but Black is very confident. You are 8 intersections from him and it is your move. Since you can capture Black only when you are one intersection from him, "parity" is with Black, and he can even approach you with impunity, allowing you to chase him all over the web, always one move behind.

Like most flies, however, Black is overconfident. You can capture him regardless of his itinerary if you divine the secret of the web. What is your strategy?

Solution to THE SPIDER AND THE FLY

If the entire web were composed of quadrilaterals, the fly would always have what checker players call "the opposition" and would be immune to capture. But there is one triangle in the web, and if you head for it and traverse its three vertices, the opposition will revert to you. Now you can start chasing Black, keeping him from going to the triangle and regaining the opposition. The pursuit will not last long, if you follow Black along "concentric" strands when possible, otherwise moving out from the center. Black can only postpone the capture, but not for long. In most cases capture will finally occur when Black is forced to move from one of the outermost strands into your double threat.

Readers are challenged to determine the maximum number of moves Black can make before the inevitable capture.

Sidegame:

In turn both Spider and Fly are permitted the option of moving to an intersection either one or two moves away from the previous position. How does this alter the outcome of the game?

79. THE TRUEL

After a mutual and irreconcilable dispute among Red, Black, and Gray, the three parties have agreed to a three-way duel. Each man is provided a pistol and an unlimited supply of ammunition. Instead of simultaneous volleys, a firing order is to be established and followed until only one survivor remains.

Gray is a 100 per cent marksman, never having missed a bull's-eye in his shooting career. Black is successful two out of three times on the average, and you, Red, are only a ⅓ marksman. Recognizing the disparate degrees of markmanship, the seconds have decided that you will be first and Black second in the firing order.

Your pistol is loaded and cocked. At whom do you shoot?

Solution to THE TRUEL

At nobody. Fire your pistol in the air, and you will have the best chance among all three truellists!

Certainly you don't want to shoot at Black. If you are unlucky enough to hit him, Gray will polish you off on the next shot. Suppose you aim at Gray and hit him. Then Black will have first shot against you and his overall probability of winning the duel will be $6/7$, yours $1/7$. Not too good.*

But if you deliberately miss, you will have first shot against either Black or Gray on the next round. With probability $2/3$, Black will hit Gray, and you will have an overall winning probability of $3/7$. With $1/3$ probability Black will miss Gray, in which case Gray will dispose of his stronger opponent, Black, and your overall chance against Gray will be $1/3$.

Thus by shooting in the air, your probability of winning the truel is $25/63$ or about 40 per cent. Black's probability is $8/21$ or about 38 per cent. And poor Gray's winning probability is only $2/9$ (about 22 per cent).

Is there a lesson in TRUEL which might have application in the field of international relations?

---

* The reader is invited to confirm Black's winning probability of $6/7$ by summing the infinite geometric series: $2/3 + (1/3)(2/3)(2/3) + (1/3)(2/3)(1/3)(2/3)(2/3) + \ldots$

80. IMPROVING THE ODDS

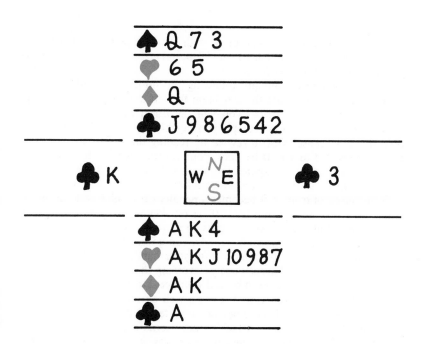

Against silent opponents, you, South, have blundered into a contract of
7 ♡. The contract is unfortunate on two counts. A small slam in hearts
is virtually unbeatable, and risking its profits in favor of the grand slam,
which bears only a 53 per cent chance of success with standard expert
play, is bad policy. Moreover, if 7 ♡ makes, so does 7 no trump.

Nevertheless, you are stuck with a 7 ♡ contract. The opening lead of
the ♣K, on which East follows with the ♣3, puts you in your hand. In
the heat of battle most experts would cash the ♡A. If either defender
failed to follow, the contract would be down one, and further play
would only be a formality. If the ♡Q dropped under the ♡A, the grand
slam would be a lay-down. If both opponents followed with low trumps,
the play for the drop would be superior to the finesse against East by
the ratio of 12 to 11 and would provide an overall success probability
of 53 per cent.

I say "most experts." However, if South has the cunning of a John
Crawford or a Helen Sobel, he will spot a line of play which will raise
those odds considerably. It's subtle but effective. Study the hands well.
Your move.

Solution to IMPROVING THE ODDS

Assuming both defenders will follow with low trumps to the first trump lead, you can raise your odds from 53 per cent to as high as 75 or 80 per cent. Here is how it is done.

While reflecting on dummy following the initial ♣K lead, you will arrange your hand so that the ♡A is on the left and next to it, the ◇K. After winning the first trick, you will lay down the ♡A. When both defenders follow with low trumps, you quickly lay down the ◇K. Your objective is to cause West to revoke by reading the ◇K as the ♡K, the card he expected to see. If he does, your contract is safe. If he revokes with a black card, he has spilled the beans regarding his singleton trump and you will go to dummy and finesse East for the ♡Q. If he revokes with the queen of trumps, it becomes a penalty card which will fall under your K on the next trump lead. If he revokes with a low trump, *that* becomes a penalty card. You will play to dummy and lead its remaining low trump. If East follows with the ♡Q, you go up with the ♡K. If East shows out, you play a low trump from your hand, and pick up West's ♡Q on the next trick, "miraculously" avoiding the loss of a trump trick with the doubly guarded queen behind your ace–king!

Does this devilish ploy work? It does, well over half the time. I have (with the connivance of the other players) tested it many times during a session of rubber bridge by stacking the alternate deck during the play of a hand. Whether the unsuspecting West was given 1, 2, or 3 trumps, and whether he was in the novice, intermediate, or expert class, he revoked more frequently than not. (Test it yourself.) Considering the singleton ◇Q in dummy and dummy's apparent lack of entries, that ◇K looks, to West, almost as much like the ♡K as the ♡K itself.

Is this sort of play ethical? Absolutely. It violates neither letter nor spirit of contract bridge law and custom. If a defender is "hustled" into a misplay by the tempo or oddness of declarer's play, he has only himself to blame.

One other point. If West follows with a diamond, you will have to decide whether he is out of trumps or just alert. I leave it to you whether, in that instance, you play for the drop or the finesse.

PART II

PART IV

Unsolved Games

The final group of games, whose solutions have eluded the author, are offered in the confident belief that nearly all of them are within the reach of sagacious readers.

Additional unsolved problems are posed as "open questions" in the Notes and Sources section.

81. REGULUS

Two players alternately connect pairs of vertices of a regular polygon with straight-line segments. No vertex may be used more than once, and no previously drawn segment may be crossed. The last player able to make a legal move wins.

In the case of a polygon with an even number of vertices, the first player wins easily by connecting opposite vertices, effectively dividing the remaining vertices into two identical groups. Now he simply replies symmetrically to each of his opponent's plays.

For polygons with an odd number of vertices, which player has the winning advantage, and what is his optimal strategy?

Sidegame:

While this book was in preparation, Gustavus J. Simmons came up with a game called SIM (*Journal of Recreational Mathematics,* April, 1969) which bears a superficial resemblance to REGULUS. Two players alternately connect vertices of a regular hexagon, each player using a different colored pencil. Any of the 15 connections may be made on a given turn, and the loser is the first player to complete a triangle with vertices corresponding to those of the hexagon and with all three segments of his own color. The reader will quickly discover that analysis of SIM is much more difficult than he may be led to believe. What is the winning strategy, and *who* has the advantage?

The game is based on Charles Bostick's clever proof that regardless of the apportionment among the two colors, after all 15 connections have been made, at least one (and, in fact, two) "chromatic" triangles will be formed. Thus a drawn game is impossible. What is particularly vexing to those who have tried to analyze SIM is the fact that the 2nd player (intuitively the favorite) cannot employ symmetry. The first player can do so, but only up to a point, at which he must abandon the symmetric strategy. One cannot use the "HEX Proof" to show that first player loses against best play, since his first segment might *not* prove to be a disadvantage. It *could* rob 2nd player of an "escape" move.

82. QUADRAPHAGE

One player is equipped with a king and allowed to move it on an infinite chessboard. The other player, the Quadraphage (square-eater), places pennies on squares and by so doing, renders them permanently off limits to the king. The players move alternately, starting with the Quadraphage, whose objective is to box in the king. He may "obliterate" any square not presently occupied by the king. The king's object is to avoid entrapment.

On a regular chessboard, with the king starting on one of the four central squares, he can always reach an outside square easily. But on the infinite chessboard, there is no hope for the king. He will eventually be trapped. The question is: How should the Quadraphage play in order to minimize the number of pennies required to box in the king?

A logical way to play this game would be to reverse the roles of the players following each game and to award the king all the pennies required to trap him.

Sidegame:
Another way to have fun with the Quadraphage concept is with a standard chessboard. The Quadraphage moves first, and his objective is to force the king to the border of the board quickly. The objective of the king, who starts in a central square, is to reach the border in the maximum number of moves. He is then awarded all the pennies required to force him to the border. The roles are reversed after each game.

The king must be careful to maintain an escape route to the border, for if he is trapped on the board, he gets no pennies.

83. LOADED DICE

Gambler Black is rolling the dice against you in the game of craps. Both of you have staked your entire bankrolls on one pass. Normally you (Gambler Red) have a slight advantage. Black wins immediately if his first roll is a "natural" (7 or 11), and loses immediately with a 2 ("snake-eyes"), a 3 ("craps"), or a 12 ("boxcars"). With any other roll (4, 5, 6, 8, 9, or 10), Black continues to roll until the spots either total 7 or the amount of his first roll. In the former case he loses; in the latter he wins.

It is not difficult to compute Black's probability of winning: $244/495$, or about 0.493, slightly less than $\frac{1}{2}$. However, Black has "loaded" one die in a manner most favorable to his cause: he has arranged that it will come up 5 100 per cent of the time, thus avoiding the possibility of snake-eyes, craps, or boxcars, and raising his probability of winning to exactly $\frac{2}{3}$.

Having learned of Black's perfidious ploy, you have the opportunity to load the other die in any manner you wish. With what probability should you load each of the six spots so as to minimize Black's chance of winning?

84. STYMIE

The vertices of a cube are to be labeled with the integers from one to eight. The two players move alternately, using any of the eight numbers to label any of the eight previously unlabeled vertices, with these two restrictions: (1) a number may not be used twice, (2) the sum of the labels of the endpoints of each edge must be *prime*. First player unable to move legally loses. (It is easy to prove that it is impossible to complete the labeling of all the vertices.) Determine who has the advantage and his optimal strategy.

85. TRIPOLEMOS

Three players, A, B, and C, holding a, b, and c chips, respectively, sit at the vertices of a triangular table. Each secretly divides his chips between his left and right hands and at a signal, all three expose their chips. The number of chips held in the left (right) hand represents the size of the force deployed against the opponent on the left (right). Between each pair of players, the one deploying the greater number of chips wins those deployed against him by that opponent. In case of a tie each retains his chips.

The game is trivial if $a = b = c$. Optimal strategy is to hold all chips in one hand, none in the other. And if coalitions are permitted, even where $a > b > c$, the optimal strategies are readily determined. Therefore we consider the game without coalitions and with a, b, and c distinct. Two versions are of interest. As a working model let the number of chips allotted the players be 3, 4, and 5.

A. The number of chips is assigned openly by lot or on a rotating basis from game to game.

B. The number of chips is assigned secretly by lot (so that no player knows which of his two opponents is the stronger).

Version B is obviously more difficult to analyze. Determine the optimal strategies, holding 3, 4, or 5 chips in both variations, and the expected number of chips each player will emerge with.

Generalize, if possible, to arbitrary $a > b > c$.

86. THE "DATING GAME"

Two players alternately tear out sheets from a loose-leaf desk calendar with the restriction that after the first move, each play must involve a date that agrees with the preceding date either with respect to number or month. The last player able to make a legal move wins. Experimentation on small "calendars" indicates that the first player has the advantage if and only if the total number of dates is odd, implying that the second player should win only if a leap-year calendar is used. Verify or disprove this conjecture.

This game lends itself to numerous generalizations and variations.

Sidegame:
Consider this simpler version: 1. First date selected must be in January. 2. Each date selected must agree with the previous date either in month or number *and* must fall later in the year. 3. Winner is the player who appropriates December 31st.

Using the SEVEN NO TRUMP technique, the reader should quickly determine the only January date that guarantees a win for the first player.

87. PEEK–A–BOO

A rectangular pattern of streets is laid out on a sheet of paper. Rather than attempt to generalize this difficult game, we will consider the case of six vertical streets, labeled A to F from left to right, and five horizontal avenues, labeled from 1 to 5, south to north. The "cat" is originally situated at the intersection of A street and 5th avenue, the "mouse" at F and 1st. The players move in turn, one block in any direction, with first move by the cat. Each player's position is unknown to his opponent, but is recorded by an umpire as in Kriegspiel Chess.

The objective of the cat is to capture the mouse. This is accomplished whenever the mouse is unfortunate enough to move to an intersection one block away from the cat's current position. Should this happen, the umpire immediately awards the cat the game.

The mouse can win only by reaching A street without previously having come within "peek-a-boo" range of the cat.

For smaller dimensions, the cat can generally win using a pure strategy. What are the optimal mixed strategies for the 5-by-6 game? Generalize if possible.

88. GRID

This game is played on an infinite square lattice, though for practical purposes a sheet of graph paper with quarter-inch grids is sufficient. The players alternately "appropriate" intersection points, the first player labeling them with circles, the second with squares. (Or two different color circles may be used.) The winner is the first player, if any, to appropriate the four vertices of a square, which may be of any size, but must be oriented in the direction of the lattice. For example, the midpoints of the sides of a two-by-two square form the vertices of an unacceptable square. What is the first player's best strategy?

89. CRAPJACK

The author originally posed the problem this way: The first player starts by placing two dice in such a way as to show any desired number of spots on top. Thereafter, play alternates with each player changing the reading of *either* die, while leaving the other die intact. After each play the total spots on *both* dice are added to the running total. The first player has the objective of bringing the aggregate total to 21 following one of his plays. Only by reaching this exact total can he win. The second player can thus win in three different ways. Say the first player starts with the dice reading 5 and 6. The second player can win by: changing 6 to 5, thereby "appropriating" 21 himself; changing 5 to 6, thereby "bypassing" 21; changing 5 to 2, thereby bringing the total to 19 and forcing the first player to bypass 21. What settings are "safe" for the first player?

By somewhat tedious analysis, the author proved that the first player loses against best defense, regardless of his initial setting. Second player seemingly has an overwhelming advantage, having three ways of beating the first player. The more general question is therefore posed: For what values of the first player's objective total N ($N > 12$) can he assure a win by choosing the proper initial setting?

Intrigued with the idea of formulating a continuous version of NIM, involving several strings of various lengths and permitting each of two players to cut off and discard a piece of any length from any one string (including the entire string), the author broke several lances in the attempt to produce a finite, nontrivial game.

Attempt A. (No restrictions.) This is not a finite game. Even if confronted with the "losing" position of two strings of equal length (allowing one's opponent to use the matching strategy) one can prolong the game past resolution by employing a decreasing sequence of cuts which converges to a length less than that of the string. (But see Notes and Sources for a challenging question.)

Attempt B. (Each cut must be at least some stipulated length, say one inch.) In this case the standard NIM solution applies with winning positions determined by simply disregarding fractional numbers of inches. For example, a leave of $1\frac{1}{4}''$, $2\frac{7}{8}''$, and π'' is a winning leave, just as $(1, 2, 3)$ is a winning leave in NIM.

Attempt C. (The cut lengths must increase from play to play.) First player has a trivial win by "cutting" the entire longest string.

Attempt D. (Each player's cut lengths must increase from play to play independently of his opponent's cuts.) Second player easily wins by taking an initial cut a few orders of magnitude smaller than that of the first player.

Final version. (Each cut must be at least as long as the current shortest string, but not as long as the next shorter string.) If this variation is either trivial or infinite, it is not apparent to the author. Given four strings of lengths 1, $\sqrt{2}$, e, and π and the option of first cut (at least one unit in length but less than $\sqrt{2}$), what initial play, if any, guarantees you the last cut? Generalize.

Allowing for the possibility that the final version is also defective, then the reader is challenged to invent a finite, nontrivial version of CONTINUOUS NIM.

91. SABAZIUS

This is a game-theoretic prelude to multipile countdown games, in which both players know the optimal game strategies. First and second player are designated beforehand, and then each player is given N counters, which he may covertly divide into any number of piles he wishes, each pile containing an arbitrary number of counters. The partitions are revealed simultaneously, and, since both players are assumed to know the countdown game strategy, the combined configuration of piles determines the winner immediately. Determine the optimum partitioning procedure for each player in games such as LASKER'S NIM, KAYLES, and GRUNDY'S GAME. The analysis for SABAZIUS as a prelude to NIM is simple (see Notes and Sources).

92. PRIME GHOST (open-ended)

First player writes one of the four one-digit primes (2, 3, 5, or 7). Thereafter, each of the two players at his turn adds a digit at either end to produce another prime. Loser is the first player to be stymied—i.e., is forced to produce a composite number regardless of what digit he adds at the left or the right of the previous prime. Who has winning advantage and what is his winning strategy?

It is interesting that in the simpler version of PRIME GHOST in which digits are added only at the right, the second player can win against any of the four openings (see Notes and Sources). One would intuitively feel that the first player was a 15-to-1 favorite.

193

93. KRIEGSPIEL TIC–TAC–TOE

Each player works on his own board, and an umpire calls "no move" whenever a player attempts to mark an occupied square. Consider three variations:

    A. A "no move" call permits a player to try another move.

    B. A "no move" call results in a loss of turn.

    C. A "no move" call results in a loss of turn for the first player, but permits the second player to try another move.

Variations A and B favor the first player strongly, and it is believed that he even has a substantial advantage in variation C. Determine the optimal mixed strategies for all three versions.

Sidegame:

The Kriegspiel concept can be extended to many popular games including GO-MOKU. Using the "A" version above, confinement of moves to a seven-by-seven grid is just about right for an interesting game. If you play it a few times, you will find that it bears a strong resemblance to the game of SALVO.

94. ESCALATION

This concept can be applied to many games, e.g.:

A. Chess version. White starts with one move; Black then has two successive moves; White, three; Black, four; etc., until the game is completed. A check may be given only on the last move of a sequence, and checkmate prior to the endgame is virtually impossible to achieve, since the responder can use all the moves to which he is entitled to counter it. Thus this is a game of attrition. Which player has the advantage?

B. Bridge version. Red and Black each selects a 13-card bridge hand as follows: from an exposed pack of 52 cards Red selects one, then Black selects two of the remaining, Red selects three more, Black selects four more, Red selects five more, and Black selects six. Finally Red completes his hand with four additional cards and Black with one.

With the two hands open, the players now bid for the contract, the defender making the opening lead. Stakes are awarded as follows: 5¢ for bidding and making a part score, 10¢ for game, 25¢ for small slam, 50¢ for grand slam, and the loss of $1 for going down.

Experimentation indicates that neither player can assure himself of a slam, but that the first player cannot be prevented from making game. Attempts to verify the latter conjecture are entertaining though difficult.

C. Poker version. Red selects one card from the exposed deck, Black selects two, Red selects three, Black selects three, and Red selects one. The hands are then compared as in showdown poker. Can Red assure himself of winning?

Preliminary analysis leads to the conclusion that with best play, the opponents will tie, either with royal flushes or with two pairs, aces and kings. However, one is liable to neglect effective but elusive moves and countermoves.

95. CHESSBOARD TRICHROME

Using chips of three different colors, two players alternately cover the squares of a chessboard with the restriction that two squares a king's move apart cannot be colored the same. Determine optimal strategies for winning (by placing the last chip).

96. CHESSBOARD CONTACT

The players alternately cover the squares of a chessboard with chips, this time with the restriction that after the first play, each square covered must be a king's move away from the last square covered. The objective is to make the last move by maneuvering into a *cul-de-sac*. Can this be done, or will best play result in the covering of all 64 squares (in which case the game is declared a tie)?

The game can be implemented using a nickel and a stack of pennies. The nickel is shifted around so as to cover the last square played.

Sidegame:
Try this violent chess variant. I call it SNOWPLOW CHESS. Bishops, castles, and queens may capture any enemy pieces in their lines of fire, ending their move on the square of the last piece captured. Their capturing forays are blocked only by pieces of their own color, the enemy king, or by the border of the board. The multiple kill capability produces a lot of fireworks, yet there appears to be quite a bit of science to the game.

97. BUY OR FOLD

The thirteen spades are shuffled, and following an ante of one chip, each player is dealt one card face up. The player with the lower ranking card may either fold and yield the antes to his opponent, or he may, for the price of one chip, purchase a new card from the pack. He may continue to buy replacements until he receives one higher than his opponent's card. Discards are all left face up and are not subsequently drawn from. If and when a player buys a card higher than his opponent's current card, the buy-or-fold option shifts to the opponent. Whenever a player folds, he loses the entire pot, including all chips paid for replacements. Under what conditions is it advisable for the low man to fold?

98. MINIPOKER

Each player is dealt one card from a pack of 52, following an initial ante of one chip. Hands rank in value from deuce up to ace with suits irrelevant as in standard poker. If a bet is called and the players hold cards of the same denomination, a tie results. The first player's options are either to fold (in which case the second player wins the antes) or to bet one chip. In the latter case, the second player may either call at the cost of one chip, in which case the hands are compared to determine the winner of the pot, or fold, in which case the first player wins the antes.

Assuming that this game is played repeatedly, only two facts are clear: players should always bet or call with an ace, and the probability with which they bet or call on a lesser hand should be an increasing function of the value of the hand.

With what probabilities should one bet or call, holding the various card denominations? If both players employ optimal mixed strategies, what is the first player's probability of winning? What is his expectation?

99. SEMI–BLIND POKER

After an initial ante of one chip each, Red and Black are dealt one card from a shuffled deck containing only a King, a Queen, and a Jack. Red looks at his card and may either fold, yielding the antes to Black, or bet four chips. If he bets, Black, who is unable to look at his own card, has four options: (a) he may fold, yielding the antes; (b) he may call at the reduced price of three chips; (c) he may pay one chip to the pot for the privilege of looking at the third, undealt card; or (d) he may pay two chips for the privilege of looking at his own card.

If Black elects option c or d, after paying and looking, he may either fold or call for four chips. What are the optimal mixed strategies, and what is Red's expectation?

Sidegame:

KING, QUEEN & KNAVE. Two players play poker with a minuscule deck consisting only of the king, queen, and jack of hearts. Each antes one chip, and dealer deals one card to each player. Receiver has two options: bet one chip or fold, yielding the antes to the dealer. If receiver bets, dealer has two options: fold, yielding the antes, or call, in which case high card holder wins the four-chip pot. Would you prefer to be in the receiver's bluffing position or the dealer's bluff-calling position? It is simple to show that receiver should always bet with king or queen and $\frac{1}{3}$ of the time with jack. Dealer should always call with king, never with jack, and $\frac{1}{3}$ of the time with queen. Dealer has a positive expectation of $\frac{1}{9}$ of a chip. The trick will be for some reader to generalize such minigames to Game 98 (MINIPOKER).

100. CHESS VARIATIONS

A. PRESTO CHESS. As originally devised, the game involved setting up the pieces as in standard chess. All chess rules apply, except for the objective: the first player to give check to the enemy king is the winner.

Though this was a challenging problem, it was found that White can win in five moves or fewer by moving QN to B3. Black must move one of three pawns to provide an escape square for his king against the threat of a knight check. White advances his knight, forcing the Black king to move, and continues by advancing the appropriate central pawn. There is no way out for Black.*

The amended version is rather more challenging: the first player to give a "safe" check (one in which the checking piece cannot be captured) is the winner. This version, of course, is not nearly so "presto" as the original version.

B. NO THREATS ALLOWED. Starting with an empty chessboard, White and Black alternately place their sixteen men, one at a time, on the board. Once placed, a piece cannot be moved. There are three restrictions. Pawns may not be placed on the top or bottom row; each player's two bishops must be placed on squares of opposite color; and no piece may be placed on a square from which it threatens or is threatened by an opponent's previously placed piece. Who has the advantage?

C. SEMI-KRIEGSPIEL. White's pieces are set up as in standard chess. Black has only his king and queen, which he may place initially on any legal squares. White, moving first, plays "blind," while Black shares the master board with the umpire, who advises White whenever he makes an illegal move, or whenever check is given or a capture is made by either side. He does not announce direction of checks or potential pawn captures.

White is impregnable if he chooses to play for a draw. He can simply move a knight back and forth. Should he settle for the draw or sally forth and play for the win?

---

* Prior to publication of *Your Move*, Martin Gardner demonstrated another elegant five-move solution employing only the two white knights.

ABOUT THE AUTHOR

David L. Silverman, educated in mathematics at Stanford, the University of Maryland and U.C.L.A., was a mathematician at Hughes Aircraft's Space Systems Division and an instructor at U.C.L.A. He was editor of "Problems and Conjectures" for the *Journal of Recreational Mathematics* and for many years chief consultant to the Litton Industries' "Problematical Recreations" series.

Notes and Sources

All games and problem settings are original with the author unless otherwise noted (except for well-known, traditional games such as chess, bridge, cribbage, etc.).

1. The author's apologies to Chileans for annexing a portion of southern Chile to Argentina. While not affecting the game strategy, it makes the map somewhat clearer.

2. In 7NT MISERE, the second player also has an assured win. The sequence of safe bids is: 3 clubs, 4 diamonds, 5 hearts, 6 no trump, and 7 spades.

3. This was an adaptation of a simpler version appearing as problem 113 in R. M. Abraham's *Diversions and Pastimes* (N.Y., Dover, 1964). By the process of "parallel invention," the game concept has also appeared as "Northcott's Nim," involving black and white pieces placed on the rows of a chessboard. (See Cedric Smith, "Compound Games with Counters," *Journal of Recreational Mathematics,* April 1968.) WOOLWORTH can be generalized to any number of tracks, each of arbitrary length. A winning position is one in which the "gap numbers" constitute a winning combination in NIM. (See game 55.)

4. If the game is played with (relatively) unorderable items, as in "Twenty Questions"—e.g., unlimited concepts such as the Eiffel Tower, the Cheshire Cat's grin, the iceberg that sank the *Titanic,* etc.—best strategy in YES OR NO is difficult to characterize.

5. Another question suggested by KING VS. KNIGHT: How many kings are required to assure capture of a lone knight?

6. By B. J. Becker (Los Angeles *Herald-Examiner*), one of the three most creative bridge-problem composers in the United States (Edwin Kantar and George Coffin being the other two), and an outstanding tournament champion.

7. To the best of my recollection, this problem is the denouement of an earlier, more complicated end position, published either in a book or in one of the checker journals, but I have been unable to rediscover the source.

8. By Martin Gardner. This is problem 2, page 23, *The Scientific*

American Book of Mathematical Puzzles and Diversions (N.Y. Simon and Schuster, 1959). Mr. Gardner remarks in the solution that following the original appearance of the problem in his *Scientific American* monthly feature, "Mathematical Games," two readers pointed out that first player can also win by selecting three 10s and two cards in the fourth suit consisting of any of the ten combinations: A-9, K-9, Q-9, J-9, K-8, Q-8, J-8, Q-7, J-7, J-6.

If the second player is permitted to draw from the first player's discards, how do you rate the latter's chance of winning?

9. Neglecting the factor of dealer's throw in hand A, the expected profit is 12.48 points with A777 and 13.04 points with 7778. The added pegging value of the first hand, together with the decreased danger of a substantial crib, far outweighs this difference.

10. The generalization of this game to three racks is unsolved. Also unsolved is the question: Given r racks, what is the largest value of N(r) for which the integers 1, 2, . . . , N can be "racked" in such a way that no rack contains two numbers together with their sum? (For r = 3, can you legally rack the integers 1, 2, . . . , 23?)

11. By Paul Lukacs and the late Robert Darvas (Hand 63 in their magnificent bridge problem anthology, *Spotlight On Card Play,* translated by Norman De V. Hart, Nicholas Kaye Ltd. [London, England, 1960]).

12. By Edwin Kantar (North Hollywood, Calif., *Valley Times*), a prolific composer of bridge problems and a strong threat to succeed Charles Goren as "Mr. Bridge" in the 1970s.

13. Although the particular hand has been fabricated, I believe that this inspired signal was actually made by Alvin Roth in tournament play, though I cannot recall the source, whether oral or printed. Or it may have been Harry Fishbein. (Perhaps both?)

14. If we assume that following a low trump lead from dummy, East is as likely as not to go up with the king, holding any king doubleton except KJ, then the chances of success for the candidate strategies are: I—34%, II—27%, III—34%, IV—27%, V—39%. What is South's best line of play at the superior contract of five diamonds? (Best contract is 3 NT.)

15. An embellishment of the classic "smother" theme (original source unknown).

16. Though the "ladder" theme is of ancient vintage, the introduction of the rook interference threats adds zest to this original.

17. If you found this to your liking, analyze the first player's best strategy if a fifth, unoccupied, row is added to the miniboard, and pawns are permitted the standard initial option of advancing one or two spaces.

18. In playing GIVEAWAY CHESS, best strategy seems to involve a cautious policy of whittling down opponent's major pieces to restrict his mobility, without exposing yourself to the danger of sequential pawn captures by one of your own major pieces. Knights play a key role: while extremely effective in the endgame, they are apt to become fatal liabilities in the midgame.

19. By Karl Fabel. This problem appears in Martin Gardner's *New Mathematical Diversions from Scientific American* (N.Y., Simon and Schuster, 1966), page 223.

20. KRIEGSPIEL problems have been a neglected field of endeavor among composers of fairy chess problems.
The KRIEGSPIEL concept can be applied to many other popular games, e.g. checkers, honeymoon bridge, dominoes, hex, and (see Unsolved Games) tic-tac-toe. [Is there a couple so devoted to the game of honeymoon bridge as to bring along a third person (the umpire) on their honeymoon?]

21. By W. Orr. This appears as problem 30 in *Beat That Neighbor at Draughts,* published by the Kilkeel Chess and Draughts Club, County Down, Ireland.

22. By A. C. Hews. This appears as problem 49 in Hews' monumental collection, *Stroke Problems* (London, Marlborough and Co., and Bristol, J. A. Kear Jr., 1917), p. 14.

23. GIVEAWAY CHECKERS, when played by experienced players, resembles the standard game closely, up till the endgame. GIVEAWAY CHESS, on the other hand, bears little resemblance to CHESS at any stage of the game. For that reason, it is superior as a change of pace from the standard game.
A strong chess or checker player, however adept he may be, if inexperienced in the GIVEAWAY versions, will invariably prove an easy mark even for an inexpert GIVEAWAY buff.

24. Because of the tremendous advantage of the geese and the generally obvious strategy of the fox (should the geese blunder into a losing

position), it is difficult to compose a truly challenging problem in this traditional game.

25. This game appeared to materialize out of thin air during the mid-fifties, and its solution was probably discovered independently by scores of players.

For entertaining discussions of TIC–TAC–TOE and many of its variations, including "the moving counter" variation, see Martin Gardner's *Scientific American Book of Mathematical Puzzles and Diversions* (N.Y., Simon and Schuster, 1959), chapter 4, and Richard A. Epstein's *The Theory of Gambling and Statistical Logic* (N.Y., Academic Press, 1967, pp. 359 ff.). Epstein mentions a variant called KIT–KAT–OAT, wherein the objective is the same as in TIC–TAC–TOE, but each player plays his opponent's personal mark. This variant is, of course, equivalent to TOE–TAC–TIC.

26. This game, which can also be styled NIM–TAC–TOE, was contributed by the author to the Litton Industries Problematical Recreations series and appeared Sept. 18, 1967, in *Aviation Week* and in *Electronic News*.

Who has the advantage if only *adjacent* squares can be marked at each turn?

27. In $3 \times 3 \times 3$ TOE–TAC–TIC first player's strategy is that of the two-dimensional version, generalized to three dimensions. Open Question: Who has the advantage in $3 \times 3 \times 3$ QUICK–TAC–TOE?

28. This increasingly popular game has been marketed by at least two manufacturers in the form of a transparent plastic framework under the names Qubic and Checkline.

29. This masterpiece and problem 28 were composed by William Porter, Hughes Aircraft Co., El Segundo, Calif.

When Mr. Porter saw his first Qubic board, in 1966, he sat down and studied it carefully. Then he challenged all comers. Since that time he has established a remarkable record among a sizable group of competitors in Southern California, both in match competition and in "move-a-day" play. Playing second, he has lost a few games, but never twice in the same way, having analyzed each loss carefully to determine where he went wrong. He has never lost playing first.

30. For an interesting discussion of HEX and three challenging problems in midget variants of HEX, see chapter ·8 of Martin Gardner's *Scientific American Book of Mathematical Puzzles and Diversions* (N.Y., Simon and Schuster, 1959).

31. As of this writing, first player's winning strategy has been determined only for HEX boards of dimensions up to 6 × 6. The number of branches in the standard 11 × 11 version remove it from the realm of profitable analysis. Unlike the case of CHESS or CHECKERS, we know that first player can always win in HEX against any play by his opponent. What would we do with the enormous printout constituting the game tree, even if there were a computer capable of providing it?

32. By Don May, Culver City, Calif. Mr. May also challenges readers to analyze the game of MICROGO, played on a 3 × 3 board. Show that the first player can guarantee a win by 8 stones. If second player can stipulate first player's initial play, where should he require him to put his first stone?

33. The rules of GO–MOKU prohibit the establishment of a fork of two open threes. This restriction was imposed because without it, it has been asserted, the game is a fairly quick win for the first player. This may well be true, though I have never seen a full analysis. Geoffrey Mott-Smith exhibits a nine-move win for the first player in the unrestricted version (*Mathematical Games for Beginners and Enthusiasts,* N.Y., Dover, 1954, p. 130), but it applies to only one of a rather large number of possible variations.

34. I believe this problem originated in the problem department of the *American Mathematical Monthly* during the forties, but have been unable to rediscover the issue or the name of the contributor.

Open Question: Is the game also a draw in three dimensions? If so, is there a value of N for which the game is a win for the first player in an N (or higher) dimensional rectangular lattice? If the answer is "yes" to both questions, what is the smallest such N?

35. By Roland Sprague. This is problem 30 in his excellent book *Recreation in Mathematics* (N.Y., Dover, 1963; translated from the German by T. H. O'Beirne).

36. Despite the well-known fact that five colors are sufficient to color any plane map and the even better-known conjecture that four colors are sufficient, generalized POLYCHROME with any desired number of colors makes an interesting game, provided the map has sufficiently many countries and sufficient contiguity.

37. The game trees resulting from other possible winning moves are probably extremely diffuse.

38. The reader should have no difficulty in showing that first player is doomed to defeat in Australian CONTACT.

39. Find first player's three winning openings in the Australian version.

40. Verify that the game is fair regardless of the values of the two coins.

41. Prove that if a payoff matrix has more than one saddle point, all have the same value.

42. How much would you bid if high bidder wins the antes and pays his opponent the amount of the *high* bid?

43. An interesting but complicated three-man game ensues if the third player is permitted to either agree or disagree with the second player. Does this game have a stable solution, assuming that the second and third players split the antes if they both announce correctly?

44. This problem stirred up a small tempest when it appeared in Litton Industries' Problematical Recreations series. The protesters unanimously attempted to show that Black and Gray will, in the long run, abandon their "dominant" strategies. But the restriction against collusion precludes this, since doing so would further their collective interests at the expense of Red's. The game has no stable solution and should not properly be considered within the realm of game theory.

If collusion is permitted, who will collude with whom and with what result? Consider two cases: silent coalitions and coalitions with conferences before each round of play.

45. The game of two-man GHOST can presumably be "laid" in the foreseeable future using computers with large enough memories to store the words of the English language or with fast access to collateral memory tapes. The basis for such optimism is that the game tree would not be too unwieldy to put into practice.

The situation is very different in the case of CHESS, CHECKERS, GO, HEX, etc. Even if computers of the far future could cope with the astronomical game trees involved in these games, thus answering the ultimate chess problem: Does White have the winning advantage, or does the game end in a draw with best play, or (most improbably) does Black have the advantage?, this would not relegate CHESS to the academic status of TIC–TAC–TOE or NIM. Since no player could hope to memorize the manifold branches, such complex games will always remain challenging to human beings.

On the other hand, experts in "heuristic programming" such as Gelernter, Killgrove, Newell, Samuel, Shaw, Simon and Slagle, have, for several years, been improving chess- and checker-playing programs which not only can delve further along the game trees than most human beings, but are also capable of "learning from their losses." "They" are already good players. During the seventies, it is not improbable that programs will have been developed in many complex games which, though imperfect, will be unbeatable by human opponents.

46. If you play first in a knockout three-man game of OPEN–ENDED GEOGRAPHY with states, can you assure that the third man will be eliminated, giving you first crack at the second player in the second (final) round?

47. The popular game of SCRABBLE is manufactured by the Production and Marketing Co.

48. Adapted from "The Game is Hot," *Recreational Mathematics Magazine,* by an outstanding composer of novel mathematical problems, Leo Moser.

49. For excellent discussions of countdown games see R. A. Epstein's *The Theory of Gambling and Statistical Logic* (N.Y. and London, Academic Press, 1967, pp. 363–82), T. H. O'Beirne's *Puzzles and Paradoxes* (N.Y., Oxford Univ. Press, 1965, pp. 130–67), and Cedric A. B. Smith's article "Compound Games and Counters," *Journal of Recreational Mathematics* (April 1968).

50. Consider this game: the player scheduled to move first writes down the initial number of counters (from 2 to N); the second player writes down the limit number of his choice. They reveal their numbers simultaneously, and the game begins. Prove that the first player's probability of winning is $\frac{k-1}{k}$, where k is the number of primes $\leqq$ N.

51. The misere version, as well as the standard game (no. 49) are both ancient. The earliest published analysis known was by Bachet around the time of the Plymouth Rock Landing, but there are many earlier references, which indicate that this simplest of countdown games probably predates TIC–TAC–TOE.

52. The original creator of this variation is unknown.

53. A traditional variation, of Russian origin.

54. Prove that if ALIQUOT is modified to preclude the subtraction of 1, then the sequence of winning leaves consists of the odd numbers and the odd powers of 2.

55. For one of the dozens of published analyses of NIM see Maurice Kraitchik's *Mathematical Recreations* (N.Y., Norton, and Dover, 1953, pp. 86–88).

56. A concise analysis is given by A. P. Domoryad, *Mathematical Games and Pastimes* (N.Y., Macmillan, 1964; translated from the Russian by Halina Moss), pp. 62–65.

57. Analyzed by Roland Sprague in *Recreation in Mathematics,* N.Y., Dover, 1963 (translated from the German by T. H. O'Beirne), pp. 49–53.
In the suggested modification in which the option of combining two piles into one is substituted for the LASKER'S NIM option of dividing one pile into two, the reader is challenged to prove that winning leaves are identical in the two games.

58. SHANNON'S NIM is analyzed in "A Mathematical Investigation of Games of 'Take-Away' " by Solomon W. Golomb, *Journal of Combinatorial Theory* (December 1966).

59. KAYLES may properly be designated DUDENEY'S NIM. That prolific puzzle creator fashioned the mathematical game from an ancient sport of the same name, which is probably the ancestor of modern bowling. (See H. E. Dudeney, *The Canterbury Puzzles,* N.Y., Dover, 1958, pp. 118–19, 220.)
Dudeney analyzed a selected position in KAYLES in the original edition of 1907 and concluded with the remark: "The complete analysis I can now leave for the amusement of the reader." "Vexation" and "bafflement" might have been more appropriate. Mathematicians "amused" themselves for nearly a half-century before achieving a complete analysis. Michael Goldberg and others worked out the winning leaves involving piles of up to twenty counters and found that pile numbers fell into classes, combinations of which constituted winning leaves. It remained for P. M. Grundy, Richard K. Guy, and Cedric A. B. Smith in the mid-fifties to prove that there were exactly eight classes, the designating numbers of which can be thought of as pile numbers in NIM. Using their techniques, mathematicians have been able to reduce many other apparently hopelessly complex subtractive games to their NIM equivalents. (See P. M. Grundy and Cedric A. B. Smith, "Disjunctive Games with the Last Player Losing," *Proc. Cambridge Phil Soc.,* July

1956, pp. 527–33, and Richard K. Guy and Cedric A. B. Smith, "The G-Values of Various Games," *ibid.*, pp. 514–26.)

60. The three references cited in note 49 all contain lucid expositions of the Grundy Function technique.

61. Suggested by the author to R. A. Epstein and discussed in his *The Theory of Gambling and Statistical Logic* (N.Y. and London, Academic Press, 1967), pp. 371–73. Solomon Golomb has shown how the sequence of winning leaves can be generated by "shift register" methods, but the question of how to recognize whether or not a number is a winning leave, without use of lengthy algorithms, remains open.

The idea of restricting the nature of the "subtractive set" can be generalized without limit to SUBTRACT–A–CUBE, SUBTRACT–A–PRIME, SUBTRACT–A–FACTORIAL, SUBTRACT–A–FIBONACCI NUMBER, etc. Moreover, the two players need not be restricted to the same subtractive set.

62. As in the preceding game, generalizations such as THE LAST BINOMIAL COEFFICIENT suggest themselves.

63. The reader is invited to determine the smallest allowable number of fingers (≥ 2) for which the second player has the advantage in THE LAST PRIME.

64. Those readers familiar with the field of experimental hybridization will have had no trouble identifying the Zock.

65. Though R. A. Epstein performed an admirable partial analysis of this nightmare creation of the author's (see *The Theory of Gambling and Statistical Logic,* N.Y. and London, Academic Press, 1967, p. 374), it is very doubtful that there is a simple formula for determining whether a given number is a winning, tying, or losing leave.

Epstein proved that every drawing position less than 20,000 is reducible to the 2-3 loop except for the loop 37-73-137-258-514-998-37, . . . , wherein only one player has the option of transferring to the 2-3 cycle.

66. Equipped with helmet, muffler, and protective padding, the author has tested his solution three times, using three different Dobermans previously unacquainted with him—two males and one female, with ages ranging from three to six years. He received many snarls and scowls, but never a bite.

67. Based on an incident on the Golden State Freeway near Newhall, Calif. The heroine was Mrs. G. R. Combs, Santa Monica, Calif.

68. This life game was suggested to the author by a similar situation involving a lady on a "frisky pony," recounted in the "What Would You Have Done?" department of *The Saturday Evening Post* and reprinted in the entertaining anthology, *Reader's Digest Teasers and Tests* (N.Y., Funk and Wagnalls, 1968), pp. 50, 145.

The solution was as follows: "I simply clamped my hands tightly over his eyes. The pony, unable to see where he was going, came to a quick stop."

The pony must have been a Shetland. Try clamping your hands over the eyes of a galloping horse, and see how far along the neck you can reach. Chances are good that you won't even be able to touch his ears.

The author's solution was put to the test in November 1968 at Sunset Ranch, Hollywood, Calif., with the permission of the owner, Julian ("Jute") Smith, a wise and successful breeder of racehorses. A horse by the name of Warlock was selected as the subject of the experiment, because he loved to run, and because he was accustomed to being "given his head" whenever he reached a certain broad and level run of about five hundred yards (known as "the stretch") on the trail leading from Sunset Stables to the Griffith Park Observatory.

As usual, Warlock started cantering when he turned into the stretch. A slight pull on the reins caused him to accelerate to a full gallop, as expected. (He regards running on the stretch as a right, rather than a privilege.)

The author removed his feet from the stirrups, placed the reins over the saddle-horn, took off his jacket, and with a sleeve in each hand, whipped it over the horse's head. Warlock braked immediately, and came to a full stop in the middle of the stretch with a minimum of stumbling, his head pulled up and kept parallel to the trail by the reins, which the author held in one hand, the jacket sleeves in the other.

The experiment could not have failed. When it comes to the instinct of self-preservation, man cannot compete with the horse.

69. Communicated to the author by Francis W. Stuckey, Portland, Oregon.

70. The "running" strategy provides odds of ½ of entering the last half of the ninth inning with a one run lead. The "safe" strategy offers a better chance of a larger lead than the former, but less than a ½ probability of emerging with any lead at all. Since one extra run is crucial, while the added value of a larger "cushion" is negligible, a game-theoretic approach, even if it were possible to determine all the necessary probabilities, is not appropriate.

71. Many armchair quarterbacks will out-think themselves on this problem. Coaches, however, are not apt to miss it.

72. The reader is invited to concoct other examples of "Tic-tac-incognito." This problem, like Leo Moser's original version of FISH SOUP (game 48), appeared in Martin Gardner's splendid monthly feature "Mathematical Games," *Scientific American.*

73. By imposing various objectives in "number gathering" games, one can produce disguised versions of many other games having a geometric structure. Is it possible, using magic cubes, to devise numerical isomorphs of three-dimensional tic-tac-toe? The problem is complicated by the fact that, in general, the "magic sum" of a magic cube can be obtained in ways which would not constitute a win in tic-tac-toe. For example, a magic cube of order three of the form:

4	12	26		20	7	15		18	23	1
11	25	6		9	14	19		22	3	17
27	5	10		13	21	8		2	16	24

cannot be used to fabricate $3 \times 3 \times 3$ TIC–TAC–TOE, using the simple rule that the first player to accumulate three numbers totaling 42 from the set 1, 2, . . . , 27 wins. Some additional restriction must be added to exclude combinations such as 10, 12, and 20, which do not form a line of the cube.

74. Can the reader generalize the standard and misere versions to the case of a revolver with N chambers?

75. What would be the fair payoff if all 52 cards are used, and the cards are laid out cyclically after each shuffle, play terminating when all four cards of any denomination have been correctly placed?

76. Adapted from a marketed version (RATE YOUR MIND PAL) described by Martin Gardner in *The Scientific American Book of Mathematical Puzzles and Diversions* (N.Y., Simon and Schuster, 1959), pp. 88–89.

For complete analysis of Sam Loyd's impossible 15 Puzzle, see Maurice Kraitchik's *Mathematical Recreations* (N.Y., Dover, 1953), pp. 302–8.

77. The reader will find it interesting to discover how the optimal allocation varies as the probability of success on each shot varies from 0 to 1.

78. This poser by Geoffrey Mott-Smith appears as problem 184

("The Carpathian Spider") in his entertaining collection *Mathematical Puzzles for Beginners and Enthusiasts* (N.Y., Dover, 1954).

79. The concept of truels has been discussed in many books and journals. The earliest appearance known to the author was in the form of a problem in the *American Mathematical Monthly*. Martin Gardner has traced it back further to Hubert Phillip's collection, *Question Time* (N.Y., Farrar and Rinehart, 1938; Problem 23).

A different version appears on pp. 56, 60–64 in Martin Gardner's *The Second Scientific American Book of Mathematical Puzzles and Diversions* (N.Y., Simon and Schuster, 1961).

Richard A. Epstein, who coined the term "truel" (triangular duel), discusses the subject in some generality in *The Theory of Gambling and Statistical Logic* (N.Y. and London, Academic Press, 1967), pp. 343–47.

80. The original architect of the "induced renege" theme is unknown.

81. REGULUS may prove vulnerable to Sprague-Grundy analysis.

Preliminary investigation indicates that the only N-gons (for $N < 19$) which present the second player with the winning advantage are those with $N = 5$, 9, or 15 vertices. These values, of course, have Grundy number zero. The five other Grundy classes so far discovered show the same mysterious lack of apparent structure as those of KAYLES.

A variation of REGULUS that permits vertices to be used as many times as desired and retains only the restriction against crossing segments allows the first player the same symmetric strategy for even N. But analysis of this variation for odd N appears to be more difficult than for the standard version by at least an order of magnitude.

82. This game was suggested by the author to R. A. Epstein, who used computer techniques to prove that if the king begins at the center of a square board of dimensions greater than 33 by 33, he cannot escape the board against a Quadraphage using optimum strategy. (See *The Theory of Gambling and Statistical Logic,* N.Y. and London, Academic Press, 1967, p. 406.)

The question still remains: what are the dimensions of the smallest square board which favors the Quadraphage?

83. It is clear that if Red loads his die so that one spot comes up 100% of the time, Black will always win. If he loads in such a way that only two faces can appear, one of them must be the 2. Then it is easy to show that his optimal loading makes the 2 come up exactly half the time and the other face (1, 3, 4, or 5) the remaining half. But this raises Black's probability from $\frac{2}{3}$ to $\frac{3}{4}$. It follows that at least three

faces must have a chance to appear. Is it possible that no weighting scheme will reduce Black's probability of $\frac{2}{3}$ and that Red should avoid tampering with the unloaded die at all?

84. The appearance of simplicity is deceptive, as the game tree branches profusely. In response to the first player's eight options, the second player has seventeen options if the first player started with 1, 2, 3, 4, 5, or 6 and sixteen if he started with 7 or 8.

85. The resemblance to "Colonel Blotto" games is only superficial. The objective (achieving force superiority without regard to attrition) is much simpler than that of the Blotto family, while the three-way nature of the battle increases the difficulty of analysis. In any event, competent game theorists can probably make short work of this problem (both variations), even generalizing to the case of N players, engaged in simultaneous pairwise conflict (POLYPOLEMOS).

86. The game can be played with a deck of cards. From the exposed deck, each player's selection must match his opponent's previous selection either in suit or denomination.
It can be generalized to any number of "properties." For example, three decks can be used, say a black, a brown, and a blue one, and each player must match the previous play either in suit, denomination, or color. Possible variations include modifying the restrictions in various ways:

A. Each play must match the previous play in *exactly* one property.
B. Each play must match the previous play in at least one property.
C. Each play must match the previous play in two properties.
D. (Antithetical version.) No play may match the previous play in any property.
E. (Misere version.) Same restriction as in A, B, C, or D, but with the objective of reserving the last legal play for your opponent.

87. To retain the feature that whenever the mouse blunders into peek-a-boo range, the cat has the next move, the mouse should have first move if the number of streets and avenues have the same parity.
Obviously, the mouse can win easily unless the number of streets exceeds the number of avenues. Two questions suggest themselves: (1.) What are the largest dimensions which permit the cat to win by a pure strategy? (2.) Can the cat's probability of winning, under optimal mixed strategies, be expressed in terms of the dimensions of the "board"?
This game, with its random walk character, may prove much easier to analyze by experts of the caliber of Rufus Isaacs than the generalized, continuous "game of pursuit."

88. Though the author has never seen an unconcluded game, first player seemingly having an overwhelming advantage, the possibility remains that the game is unwinnable under optimal play.

89. It is simple to demonstrate that for $N = 13$, the first player assures a win with the initial setting $(1,1)$. In view of the first player's stringent objective, it is probable that there is a maximum value of N for which he can assure a win. If so, the reader is invited to find it and to generalize to dice with k spots, and, perhaps, even with respect to the number of dice.

90. In attempt A it was observed that the game is not finite. However, though at first glance it appears to have the cardinal of the continuum, the number of possible rounds is, in fact, denumerable. Therefore, if we stretch the concept of "game" to allow it to be played by immortals with sufficient patience to play *aleph nought* rounds, then in a sense, a player "wins" if he can confront his opponent with two strings of equal length. What would constitute a winning cut if one is confronted with three strings of length l, e, and π? Benjamin L. Schwartz of MITRE Corporation has solved this "game" by generalizing the standard NIM solution to negative powers of two. Thus a winning leave is one in which the number of 1's in each binary "decimal" position of the string lengths is even. Schwartz, with justice, is unwilling to regard this version as a "game" and feels he has provided the solution to a nonexistent problem.

In the "final version" of CONTINUOUS NIM, in which each cut must be at least as long as the shortest string, but *shorter* than the next shortest, the reader is invited to verify that if there are only two strings, one's opponent will lose if confronted with the case in which the ratio of the longer string to the shorter is less than the "golden ratio"

$$\frac{1 + \sqrt{5}}{2}$$

91. In NIM SABAZIUS, one notes first that any partitioning of N counters will always be equivalent, in NIM value, to a single pile with the same parity as N, and that among the various partitions all such values from 0 to N (N even) or from 1 to N (N odd) can be obtained. Since the second player wins only by matching the value of his opponent's partition, his chance of winning is $\frac{1}{k+1}$, where k is the largest integer $\leq N/2$ (assuming each player acts optimally by selecting each value randomly with equal probability).

For lack of a better name, Sabazius ("breaker into pieces"), a sobriquet of the wine god Dionysus, was chosen for this game.

92. In the closed-end version of PRIME GHOST, second player wins immediately against the opening of 5. He converts to 53 (no three-digit prime begins with these two digits). Against 7, play proceeds 71-719-7193-71933-719333, second player winning. (Each of the first player's responses was forced.)

Against 2, play proceeds 29-293-2939-29399-293999-2939999-29399999. Against 3, second player responds 37. If first player responds 379, second player wins with 3793. If instead he responds 373, 3733 follows, and first player again has two options: 37339 loses to 373393, and 37337 loses via 373379-3733799-37337999.

It is clear that solution of the open-ended version will require the services of a high-speed digital computer. Apart from the large number of branches expected, no existing table of primes can cope with the giant numbers which will appear in the game tree.

It has been pointed out that since a "word" is not completed, so long as it is prime, the game is more properly designated "Composite Ghost."

93. This game was suggested by the author to R. A. Epstein and is discussed briefly on page 362 of his *The Theory of Gambling and Statistical Logic* (N.Y and London, Academic Press, 1967).

94. In the Gin Rummy version of ESCALATION the sequence of selection is 1-2-3-4-5-5-4-1. Can either player guarantee himself a "gin" hand while denying one to his opponent?

Among other games which lend themselves to the ESCALATION variation are Go, Salvo, Chinese Checkers, and Backgammon.

95. This game invites generalization to N-by-N boards and to C colors, but fruitful analysis will probably require investigation of miniversions (N < 8 and C < 3).

96. Both this and the preceding game invite consideration of alternative restrictions based on chess pieces other than the king. If the knight's move is used in CONTACT, the objective is to make the terminating move of an interrupted "Knight's Tour."

97. At first glance, it would seem that either player has the same chance of buying the ace if that card was not dealt originally and, therefore, the low man should always fold immediately, rather than be the first player to "sweeten the pot."

This, of course, is not the case. If high man is dealt the king, low man is certain to buy the ace eventually, winning back his purchase chips plus the antes. On the other hand, if high man is dealt the queen, low man should fold, since he has an even chance of buying the ace (and winning one chip) or buying the king (losing his ante plus all the chips he paid for it).

98. A tough game to analyze, probably requiring the combined talents of an experienced game theorist and a digital computer.

99. With only three cards to contend with, one tends to regard the game as less difficult than it actually is. The game matrix is discouragingly large.

100. A. This game was devised by Lawrence S. Crane of Los Angeles, and the solution to the original version was provided by Walter Penney, Greenbelt, Md.

B. In practice, best play appears to involve placing the most powerful pieces first. However, the work factor involved in analyzing this game appears forbidding, even with the benefit of a high-speed digital computer.

C. In actual play, White seems to have the capability of queening enough pawns to zero in on Black without suffering serious attrition. The reader is challenged to design a safe, indefensible program of attack for White, bearing in mind the possibility that Black may attempt a stalemate. If he succeeeds, he is awarded a "moral" victory.

Bibliography

Abraham, R. M., *Tricks and Amusements*, N.Y., Dover, 1964.

Ball, W. W. Rouse, *Mathematical Recreations and Essays* (revised by H. S. M. Coxeter), N.Y., Dover, 1987.

Beat That Neighbor at Draughts, County Down, Ireland, the Kilkeel Chess and Draughts Club.

Darvas, Robert and Paul Lukacs, *Spotlight on Card Play* (trans. by Norman De V. Hart), Long Island City, N.Y., Barclay Bridge Supplies Co., 1960.

Domoryad, A. P., *Mathematical Games and Pastimes* (trans. by Halina Moss), N.Y., Macmillan, 1964.

Dudeney, H. E., *The Canterbury Puzzles,* N.Y., Dover, 1958.

Dunn, Angela, *Mathematical Bafflers*, N.Y., Dover, 1980.

Epstein, Richard A., *The Theory of Gambling and Statistical Logic,* N.Y., Academic Press, 1967.

Gardner, Martin, *The Scientific American Book of Mathematical Puzzles and Diversions,* N.Y., Simon & Schuster, 1959.

———, *The Second Scientific American Book of Mathematical Puzzles and Diversions,* N.Y., Simon & Schuster, 1961.

———, *New Mathematical Diversions from Scientific American,* N.Y., Simon & Schuster, 1966.

Golomb, Solomon W., "A Mathematical Investigation of Games of 'Take-Away,' " *Journal of Combinatorial Theory,* December 1966.

Greenblatt, M. H., *Mathematical Entertainments,* N.Y., Crowell, 1965.

Grundy, P. M. and Cedric A. B. Smith, "Disjunctive Games with the Last Player Losing," *Proc. Cambridge Phil. Soc.,* 52, Part 3, July 1956.

Guy, Richard K. and Cedric A. B. Smith, "The G-Values of Various Games," *ibid.*

Hews, A. C., *Stroke Problems,* London, Marlborough & Co. and Bristol, J. A. Kear, 1917.

Kraitchik, Maurice, *Mathematical Recreations,* N.Y., Dover, 1953.

Mott-Smith, Geoffrey, *Mathematical Puzzles for Beginners and Enthusiasts*, N.Y., Dover, 1954.

O'Beirne, T. H., *Puzzles and Paradoxes*, N.Y., Oxford Univ. Press, 1965.

Phillips, Hubert, *Question Time*, N.Y., Farrar & Rinehart, 1938.

Reader's Digest Teasers & Tests, N.Y., Funk & Wagnalls, 1967.

Smith, Cedric A. B., "Compound Games with Counters," *Journal of Recreational Mathematics*, April 1968.

Sprague, Roland, *Recreation in Mathematics* (trans. by T. H. O'Beirne), N.Y., Dover, 1963.

Additional References

Game Theory:

Dresher, Melvin, *The Mathematics of Games of Strategy*, N.Y., Dover, 1981.

McKinsey, J. C. C., *Introduction to the Theory of Games*, N.Y., McGraw-Hill, 1952.

Williams, J. D., *The Compleat Strategyst*, N.Y., Dover, 1986.

(For additional mathematical approaches to the subject of games, see Richard A. Epstein's comprehensive bibliography in *The Theory of Gambling and Statistical Logic*.)

Chess, Checkers, and Bridge (of the scores of published collections of problems, only a few of the author's favorites are listed).

Chess:

Abrahams, Gerald, *Test Your Chess*, N.Y., London House & Maxwell, 1963.

Chernev, Irving, *Chessboard Magic*, N.Y., Dover, 1960.

Howard, Kenneth S., *Spectacular Chess Problems*, N.Y., Dover, 1965.

Reinfeld, Fred, *Strategy in the Chess Endgame*, N.Y., Cornerstone Library, 1964.

White, Alain C., *Sam Loyd and His Chess Problems*, N.Y., Dover, 1962.

Checkers:

Boland, Ben, *Masterpieces in the Game of Checkers,* Brooklyn, N.Y., Ben Boland, 1947.

Denvir, John T., *Traps and Shots,* Chicago, John T. Denvir, 1905.

Grover, Kenneth M., and Tom Wiswell, *Let's Play Checkers,* N.Y., David McKay Inc., 1964.

Ryan, William F., *Scientific Checkers Made Easy,* N.Y., Winston, 1934.

Wales, G. F., *Puzzler Series* (A,B,C,&D), Buffalo, N.Y., G. F. Wales, 1954.

Bridge:

Coffin, George S., *Sure Tricks,* London, Faber & Faber, 1952.

Erdos, Ivan, *Bridge à-La-Carte,* Los Angeles, American Press, 1966.

Kempson, Ewart and Paul Lukacs, *Single Dummy Plays,* Long Island City, N.Y., Barclay Bridge Supplies, 1962.

Perkins, Frank H., *Vital Tricks,* Waltham, Mass., George S. Coffin, 1953.

Reese, Terence, *Play Bridge with Reese,* N.Y., Barnes & Noble, 1962.